Everything I Never Wanted to Be

*A memoir of
alcoholism and addiction,
faith and family,
hope and humor*

Dina Kucera

Dream *of* Things

Downers Grove Illinois USA

Published by Dream of Things
Downers Grove, IL
dreamofthings.com

Kucera, Dina.
    Everything I never wanted to be : a memoir about alcoholism and addiction, faith and family, hope and humor / Dina Kucera.
    p. cm.
    ISBN 978-0-9825794-3-5
1. Kucera, Dina. 2. Alcoholics–Family relationships–United States–Biography. 3. Alcoholics–United States–Biography. 4. Drug addicts–United States–Biography. 5. Drug abuse–United States–Biography. 6. Recovering alcoholics–United States–Biography. 7. Comedians–Biography. I. Title.

HV5293.K83
362.29/2/09–dc22   2010929265

Cover designed by: Megan Kearney, Cartwheel Design Studio
Book designed by: Susan Veach

First Dream of Things Edition

Everything I Never
Wanted to Be

This book is for John and my girls.
In the end we may only have pieces of a great life.
But those pieces really kick ass.

Contents

Acknowledgements

My husband, my daughters, my grandson, and my mother… thank you for all the material. Good and bad. Mike O'Mary… thank you for being the one who said yes, after seventy-four people said no. Thank you, thank you for your patience and editing and believing in me and publishing this little book. Mark Shelmerdine, thank you for being my mentor and friend. I do not believe I would have been able to continue forward without your encouragement and support. Thank you could never convey how grateful I am. Thank you my sister Lisa for making me laugh and think and "suggesting" that I smooth out the rough edges. Which often included lengthy vile rants that were heavily peppered with the F word. Thank you to the random people that have come in and out of my house with warrants, in ankle bracelets, and high, drunk, or detoxing. You looked me right in the face, grinding your teeth and falling asleep in mid-sentence, and attempted to explain the problem with trucks that don't have cup holders large enough to hold a Big Gulp, and in the next breath wondered what we can do about the kids in orphanages in the Hamptons. And last, but sort of first, thank you stand-up comics across the country for making me laugh when I really didn't have anything to laugh about. From the top to the bottom of this list, I truly love you all. I get far more than I give. Thank you.

Prelude

The doctor rolls the stethoscope over my stomach and then stops. He says, "See. Right there. Can you hear it?"

I listen. Then, as clear as day, I hear your heartbeat. It is confirmation that you are with me and I am with you.

As I listen, I try to picture you and what you will be like. And I know that whatever the future may bring, I will always be comforted by the sound of your heart.

I'm okay with the fact that I always give up.

I have a hard time believing I will ever have a good life.

I leave my family for people who don't care about me.

I don't have any real friends.

I'm attracted to the ugliest of people.

I've learned to like the violent fucked-up life style.

Shooting speed always comes first. It's not up to me anymore.

I share needles.

I'm a cutter.

I'd rather be in pain.

I'm okay knowing I will die. It won't take long.

I feel like I'm alive to show people what happens to those who never stop.

In some sick way I enjoy not knowing if I'll make it through this shot.

I have decided that when I get caught doing something by the police I will kill myself right away.

I've destroyed my family.

I have become everything I never wanted to be.

Carly

sixteen years old

The Funniest Mom
in America

I was doing the Funniest Mom in America TV show at the Laugh Factory in Los Angeles. They announced my name, so I got this burst of energy and ran up on the stage like I normally do.

I grab the microphone and…nothing. I stand there, staring at the audience. You could hear a pin drop. The longer I stare, the longer they stare.

Some young girl in the front row screams, "Boo! Get her off!"

I've been doing this for eighteen years! What the hell is going on? I could tell them about my day job as a grocery store checker, or about the family that lives under my mother's bed, or about how my grandson's leg brace gives him super powers, or the time my husband attacked a drug dealer with a stick, or how a caseworker suggested Cosmic Bowling as a way to treat my teenage daughter's heroin addiction, or the time I got drunk and gave my car away, or my stay in a mental hospital, or anything about life in a family full of alcoholism, addiction and mental illness—all of which sounds tragic, but to a stand-up comic, it's a never-ending source of material. But no. I say nothing.

The young girl boos again. I see my daughter, Jennifer, in the back of the room, half standing, like she might jump on the horrible screaming woman.

It seems like seven hours later when a joke finally comes out of my mouth and I get rolling a little bit. But the damage is done. I am officially not the Funniest Mom in America.

My daughter, Carly, has been in and out of drug treatment facilities since she was thirteen. Every time she goes away, I have a routine: I go through her room and search for drugs she may have left behind. We have a laugh these days because Carly says, "So you were look-ing for drugs I might have left behind? I'm a drug addict, Mother. We don't leave drugs behind, especially if we're going into treat-ment. We do all the drugs. We don't save drugs back for later. If I have drugs, I do them. All of them. If I had my way, we would stop for more drugs on the way to rehab, and I would do them in the parking lot of the treatment center."

I'm fumbling around, going through Carly's things piece by piece. I look in books, shoes, jacket pockets, DVD cases. I look in holes in stuffed animals. I see a box in the top corner of her closet. I open the box and see piles of papers.

I shuffle through them and see cute little cards, letters from friends, funny little notes from her old life. "Dear Justin. Do you like me? I like you. If you don't like me it's okay. But I will not be your friend." Ribbons, stickers, and glitter line the bottom of the box.

*Then I find this…this list of what Carly feels about herself.
I read and my heart begins to beat really fast. Toward the end of
the list, I have to blink to allow the tears to roll down my face so
I can see.*

*I am holding in my hand the truth. There are a million
ways to get to the truth. The shittiest way to find the truth is to
stumble upon it accidentally while sparkly glitter falls all over
your lap.*

The last few years, I thought Carly was just going through a stage.
It was a nightmare that would end some day, and it wasn't as bad
as I thought. But Carly simply could not stay clean. She would use
meth to get off heroin, and then use heroin to get off meth. I have
become so desensitized to drug use that I would feel much better
if I thought Carly was high all day and having the time of her life.
But that's not how it was.

Of the three times Carly was in intensive care, one of those
times was a suicide attempt. The fact that her drug use made her
so sad that she didn't want to be alive anymore broke me in half.

The day Carly tried to commit suicide, she came to me and
told me she couldn't live the rest of her life as a drug addict. She
had just taken every drug she could get her hands on. Heroin,
Xanax, OxyContin, Fentanyl. She had a variety of drugs in the
house, and she had taken all of them.

*I take Carly to the emergency room. She tries to tell them
what she has taken, but she can hardly speak. They immediately
admit her. They have a nurse sit by her bed twenty-four hours a
day in case Carly goes into cardiac arrest.*

Three days into her stay, Carly begins having seizures. It is a horrible thing to watch. I ask when the seizures will stop. The doctor says they may stop, they may not. It depends on what level of damage she has done to her brain.

When a seizure starts, Carly's eyes flicker and her head falls all the way back, as if her neck will break. She can't talk. This happens every half hour or so.

I sleep in the hospital in a chair next to her bed. Late one night, Carly wakes up and looks at me. She looks like a little girl. A pretty, pretty little girl. The room is dark except for the light coming from the nurse's laptop computer, but I can still see Carly's face and striking green eyes.

She is slurring her words, but I'll never forget what she says: "I wish I was like other girls. The girls who go to the mall or to the movies. They're all bright shiny stars. And I'm like this. I don't have a best friend. I don't have any friends."

Carly rolls over facing away from me, begins to fall asleep, and mumbles, "They're all bright shiny stars." As she speaks, I can feel my heart crumbling.

The hospital stay happened to fall the week before I had go be the Funniest Mom in America. I told my husband, John, I shouldn't go. He said I would hate myself if I didn't, and that I couldn't cancel on such short notice. So I decided to go. But I had slept on a chair for a week in the hospital and had to be in Los Angeles the following day. I didn't feel great, so Jennifer drove me.

We got a room in the ghetto because it didn't look like the ghetto in the picture on the Internet. The picture on the Internet had a beautiful family sitting poolside drinking exotic drinks.

That family was not there, and the view from the only window in our room was of what we eventually figured out was a payday loan store—although we couldn't be sure because the sign was in Spanish. As a matter of fact, every business in that area had a sign that was in Spanish. That explained why when Jen and I walked into the motel lobby, the illegal immigrant desk clerk backed up against the wall with his hands up.

I said, "We have a reservation."

He put his arms down and breathed a sigh of relief. "They have reservation. Oh my Got. That scare the sheet out of me."

We were scared, too. The Internet also said you could "walk to shopping" from our motel. Any time you stay at a motel that advertises, "Walk to shopping," be afraid. If we were shopping for crack cocaine, they were right, we could walk. Probably down the hall.

Jen and I both wake up the morning of the big funny event with fevers. I am so dizzy I can't get out of the bed, so we both go back to sleep to the sound of gunshots and police sirens.

Jen gets me to the comedy club where the other funny moms are already waiting to go on. I still have a fever and am dizzy. All the moms are pacing back and forth, thinking about all the funny things they are going to say, but I am thinking about Carly. I have my cell phone in my hand the entire time, calling and checking on her every fifteen minutes. One time, I get her on the phone. Carly says, "Just be funny. You can do this, Mom."

I get off the phone, and I am pacing back and forth, completely blown away that only a week ago, such a beautiful, intelligent, amazing person tried to commit suicide. And I am that person's mother. The tears come and I sneak out the side door and walk around the corner of the club to shake it off. Then I put on a smile and walk back in. My hands are shaking from the image of Carly and the sound of her voice.

A few moms go on before me and it's almost my turn, and I suddenly realize I should have also been pacing and thinking of funny things like the other moms had been doing. But I didn't and now here I am. On stage. Unfunny. I think of something funny, but then I have a tiny flash of Carly having a seizure and my stomach rolls with anxiety. I have been a comic for eighteen years and I have never felt so unfunny in my life.

I do my silent set. I am like a mime that doesn't do any mime movements. I'll remember that the next time the joke doesn't come out. Just mime "Trapped in a Glass Box."

I look at the other moms afterwards. I'm sure they are funny all the time. I can see the women and their husbands and kids just laughing and laughing all day and night. I bet not one of them has a seventeen-year-old at home shooting up heroin. Not that they know of at least.

Jen and I are driving home the next day, and I can't stop ranting about what happened the night before.

Jen says, "It's okay, Mom. You're not the Funniest Mom in America. But you are the Funniest Mute in America."

Welcome to My Life

See, this is actually my life. I'm not a writer. I'm a checker in a grocery store. I'm surrounded by these strange people who claim to be my family. My crappy leased house is on the busiest street in Phoenix, and I can hear the traffic and ambulances like they're driving through my living room. When I hear a cop siren, I check to see if they're stopping at my house, and then I'm relieved when they pass to go and ruin someone else's day. My life really starts when I get home from work, but first, I have to spend eight hours checking on the express lane...eight hours smiling at idiots.

My customer counts out ninety-six cents in change. "Can I get rid of this?"

Of course you can. The express lane is the perfect place to unload your enormous pile of change.

Ten items or less. It ain't brain surgery. I wish I had a dime for every person who says, "I might be just a few items over the limit." Forty items later, I'm still scanning—and because I haven't evolved into the person I want to be, I scan slowly so the other people in line can burn holes in my customer's head with their angry eyes. I smile and scan and say a prayer that God will help me be a better person after this order.

At least twice a day someone says they did my job in high school. What they are saying is that when they were a dumb teenager, they did my job before they became an important member of society. I just smile and act interested.

When I get a break, I sit outside on the tiny bench that is the only place designated for smokers in the giant parking lot. I light my cigarette and Random Man passes by. He says, "Good morning. The Dow is down thirteen points."

This man always has a fact to give me. He comes in two or three times a day. He's a very nice man so I act really interested: "Thirteen points? That is ridiculous."

I go in the store and I start scanning things. Millions of things. It never ends. I scan about a thousand things and then I look at the clock. I've been at work five minutes. I look down, scan more, and wonder at what point my life veered this horribly off course. Then I remember and keep scanning.

I say to a customer, "Two dollars and twenty-nine cents."

She says, "What! What did I buy!" I hear this twenty times a day.

I say, "You bought cheese."

She shakes her head and hands me the money. "You may as well hold me at gun point."

I think, For cheese?

The next customer: "No, no, no! That was ninety-nine cents! Go look at it!"

I go look at it. It's three dollars.

"You're robbing me. I'll shop somewhere else!"

I think, I really hope she doesn't shop anywhere else.

The next customer walks up smiling about the previous customer. He says, "Some people are crazy. I know because I did your job in high school."

A girl walks up on her cell phone, acts like I'm invisible, and then says, "Thanks, Sweetie." The girl is younger than my kids.

Random Man has finished his shopping. He walks by and says, "Did you know that koala bears eat rubber?"

I say, "Really? Rubber? That...is...crazy."

He says, "Yeah. See you later."

I look at the clock. I've been at work ten minutes. I scan for two hours, and then I go back and sit on the bench for ten minutes. Not eleven. Ten.

I light a cigarette and a customer walks by and shakes his head. "You should not be smoking. My brother smokes and now he talks through a tube in his neck and urinates blood." I have absolutely no response to this.

I see he's holding a plastic bag with a giant bottle of scotch. I think I should tell him that he shouldn't drink because my brother drank scotch, then he lost his wife and kids, and now he lives in an asylum shitting his pants all day. But I don't say that because I'm a Christian. Thank you, God, he finally walks off. I have two more minutes. I walk back in the store, and the manager says, "Finally. You were gone for thirteen minutes."

I'm thinking, Suck my ass, but I say, "Wow. Really? I'm sorry. I must have lost track of those three minutes."

I get a huge order and ask a bagger to help me. He walks over with his pants sagging down halfway across his ass. He's texting on his phone. The groceries come down the belt, and he stares off into space dropping things in the bags. He has two speeds. Stopped. And slower than fuck.

I feel really irritated. I end up bagging most of the order myself. I look at the clock and I've been back from my thirteen minute break for five minutes.

Eight hours later I finally walk out the door and run into Random Man. I say good night.

He says, "They say that unemployment in Detroit is up thirty-six percent."

I say, "Thirty-six? This is insane. Okay, well, have a good night."

I drive home with every single ounce of life completely sucked out of me.

Ten years. I have been scanning bologna for ten years. The only possible way in hell that this will not feel like I've completely wasted ten years of my life is if I'm ever in my wildest and most insane dreams on Oprah and she says, "I wonder what koala bears eat?"

I will immediately say, "Rubber. They eat rubber, Oprah."

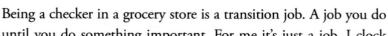

Being a checker in a grocery store is a transition job. A job you do until you do something important. For me it's just a job. I clock in, I scan, I clock out, I go home. That's when I start my real job. Home sweet home.

I get home and my grandson, Moses, is there. He smiles and comes right away to give me some love and kisses.

Moses is eight, but because he has cerebral palsy he can't balance on the toilet and he's terrified of the potty training process. Consequently, he's not potty trained. And just my luck, I walk in right after he's wet through his jeans.

Moses can't talk but we have a whole language that we understand with him coupled with sign language. Moses is very clear about what he wants, and just like any other eight-year-old, he wants it now.

My mom also lives with us. She has Parkinson's Disease. Mom hallucinates and is not alert most of the time. She mumbles, and when you say, "What Mom?" she'll scream, "Are you deaf?!"

Once when I was holding her up off the toilet, with my spine about to snap and the muscles in my shoulder ripping, she says, "It's getting to where I can't even wipe myself anymore." Then she looks up at me with her wild eyes and says, "That's good news for you."

I hear Mom ringing her bell, and I walk into her room, still in my work uniform. We are the only people in her room, but she motions for me to come closer.

She whispers, "There's a conspiracy."

"What are you talking about, Mom?"

"A conspiracy. There's a conspiracy."

"Okay. I'll check it out."

"Thank you. I've had to wait all day to tell you that."

"Okay."

"Don't tell anyone about it."

"Okay. I..."

"Keep your voice down."

I whisper, "Okay."

My house is like living with the circus. All we need is a midget and a bearded lady. Well, all we need is a midget.

John has been out of work, so he has been following behind everyone in the house and shutting off lights literally when you're still in the room. He lost his job and can't find work so they repossessed our car. If I don't work enough hours at my job, they cancel our health insurance. The bill collectors call nonstop, so now I answer the phone and when they ask for me I say I'm deceased.

Moses comes around the corner with a Coke can that he's gotten from God-knows-where. I grab it and get him a juice box. He shakes his head "no" because he wants the Coke, not the juice.

John says, "How can we afford those juice boxes? What are they, like three dollars?"

I don't respond and give Moses his juice. He takes a big drink and smiles at Grandpa as if to say, "The economy is not my problem, Grandpa."

My oldest daughter, Jennifer, walks in with her girlfriend and says to John, "I have to borrow twenty dollars for gas or I can't get to work."

John says, "What exactly don't you people get? I. Don't. Have. Any. Money."

In private, I give Jen a twenty and tell her she has to take the transaction to her grave.

An hour later, Jen goes to the emergency room because she says her heartbeat is skipping. She says it's a heart attack for sure and she can't stop itching. She says she's probably been bit by something that is giving her the heart attack, and then she's out the door to get medical treatment.

My middle daughter, April, calls me and says someone took her Grammy CD out of her case and she wants it back. I tell her she may have misplaced it. Of course she didn't misplace it. Her CDs are all categorized and in alphabetical order. She could feel the weight in this particular case was off and sure enough, the Grammy CD is gone. She says she has to go because if she

dries her shirts for more than twenty-seven minutes, they aren't
right and she has to rewash them.
    She says, "Shit. My twenty-five minute timer went off."
    Click, the phone goes dead.

I have adult attention deficit disorder with bi-polar characteristics, coupled with obsessive compulsive disorder. Jen is bipolar with a panic disorder. April has post-traumatic stress disorder with some OCD on the side. Carly, my youngest daughter, is bipolar, OCD, ADD with a splash of PTSD on top. I tell the girls that sometimes when they talk, it's like their brains spin really fast in one direction, and then abruptly stop and spin in the other direction.

A typical statement from Carly sounds like, "I'm full. I want to be a nurse. Do you like gummy worms? I want to go to interior design school. Motorcycles are loud. Did you just see a flash of light? I'm starving." The brain, spinning and spinning.

Then Jen says, "I'm having a panic attack. Or a heart attack. Or liver failure. What is this lump? I don't have a lump on my other shoulder. Now I'm depressed."

April says, "Of course you're depressed. Your glasses are mixed with your cups, and your plates are where your bowls should be. I'm sorry but how do you people live this way?" The brain still spinning and spinning like tornados in our heads.

If you want to see the underbelly of mental health disorders colliding, you should see us on a trip.

Carly stands at the edge of the boardwalk in sweats that
say "Juicy" across the ass. She looks out onto the ocean and
begins to cry. She says, "It's so beautiful." Then suddenly she

stops crying and with a tear still running down her face, says, "Do I smell pizza?"

We get to the pizza stand and Jen says, "Mom, you know CPR right? I mean seriously, you may have to give me CPR sometime today. I'm having chest pains. I also think I have liver damage."

I say, "Okay. I'll save you."

Then I say to April, "Get me a slice of cheese."

April says, "Wait. What is the system here? Are there two lines or one? There should be a place-your-order line and a pick-up-your-food line. Excuse me, sir? We should have two distinct lines. Are you placing an order or picking up an order?"

Carly: "I wish this pizza was a cheeseburger."

Jen: "My arm is numb. Would a stroke take this long?"

April: "Are you kidding me? This table isn't clean. Excuse me, sir! Who's in charge of wiping down the tables?" He says nobody. April says, "Okay! Thanks!" Then looks down and mumbles, "Fucking idiot."

I say, "Can we just sit and have a nice lunch? The ocean is beautiful...the day is beautiful."

April: "Why do I feel irritated when you talk? Really, Mom. The second you open your mouth, I know you're going to say something that gets on my nerves."

"Because you think you hate me right now? It will go away, Sweetie."

"No, it won't. And 'Sweetie'? Really?"

Jen: "I think I just went blind in my left eye."

Carly crying, "You guys just don't get it!" Laughing with tears running down her face: "I don't know why I said that."

April: "Jesus Christ. We're going to get food poisoning or

the Ebola Virus or something. This pizza is probably our last fucking meal."

Jen: "Okay! I'm already starting to feel it! I've got the Ebola
Virus. Or a tumor."

April: "You may have Salmonella."

Me: "Girls, please stop!"

I am magic. I'm the only person in the house who can wave my
hand and make mysterious people go away.

Mom rings her bell. I hear an ambulance drive by the house
as I walk into her room.

Mom says, "Did you take care of it?"

"The conspiracy? Yes. I did."

"Thank God. Now, can you bring me a root beer? I'm going
to rearrange everything in my drawers."

"Okay."

She leans toward me and whispers, "Also. That man is
under my bed smoking a cigar. Can you get him out of here?
Cigar smoke makes me queasy."

"Okay." I lean down and wave my hand under the bed.
"Okay. He's gone."

Once John tried to make the cigar man go away. Mom said,
"All he did was aggravate him." The cigar man, the little girl, the
family with several children who sleep with Mom and cause her
to worry about rolling over on one of the kids...I wave my hand
and they are gone. Magic.

There have been several times when Mom has accused me of

trying to poison her. She looked at me and said, "Just what are you trying to pull here?" As if with all the drug knowledge I've been forced to retain in my head, I wouldn't know how to get her to heaven the first time out. As if I would wait until I've given her showers for four years. I love her but she is sucking the life out of me. Quickly.

My sweet Moses follows me everywhere I go. If I stop, he runs into me and then laughs. Man, I love Moses. I love him so much I can't stand it.

--- ❧ ---

It's two weeks before Christmas and for the first time ever, we've canceled Christmas. The only person who is getting a present is Moses.

We canceled Christmas because of the economy. I think we should buy a big white van and drive to Mexico once a day and drop off a bunch of white people. Sorry, but there are no jobs in our country.

Because there are no jobs in our country, my brother in-law, Geo, just moved in with us. So it feels like there are sixteen people living in our house. It's only a temporary situation. Until the economy gets better. Jesus Christ.

John and Geo are identical twins. So now there are two of them sitting in the living room. I was fine with just the one. I walk in each day and there they are. The twins. The boys. Right there on the couch watching sports. Even with the bad economy, we still have two hundred sports channels, so there is a big sporting event on all day long. Holy God Almighty.

--- ❧ ---

John and I have been married twenty years and I adore his family. He has six siblings…all funny and creative.

When John's mother passed away, John and his brothers drove from Phoenix to Chicago to bring their father and all his belongings back to Phoenix to live with John's sister, Cheryl.

They pull up in an enormous U-Haul. A very small part of the U-Haul is their father's belongings. Most of it is "collections." Hundreds of collections.

It is unbelievable. They pull them out of boxes, one after another. Thimble collection. Cat collection. Egg collection. I watch this and am blown away. Maybe because we were always so poor that financing a collection of any sort would have meant we wouldn't have electricity.

Here's the part that made this strange event hysterical: all the siblings began to fight.

"Why should you have the Beanie Baby collection? You already took the ceramic head collection."

"I took the ceramic head collection because it will look nice in my living room."

"Fine. If you take the Beanie Baby collection, I'll take the bell collection."

"So take the bell collection. I'll take the glass egg collection."

"Why are you so selfish? It's supposed to be fair. You're such a fucking asshole. Just take the fucking eggs."

"No, fuck you. You take the eggs and I'll take the ceramic cats."

"I'm the one who helped Mom collect the fucking ceramic cats! Just fuck off! Take the eggs and the cats and shove them up your ass."

"Shove the Beanie Babies up your ass."

"You know what, you whore? Why don't you go have another abortion?"

"Fuck off. At least I wasn't in prison, you filthy sack of shit. And now, I'm taking the ceramic produce collection whether you like it or not, you fucking piece of fucking dog shit! Come on! Come get me! It'll be the sorriest day of your life, motherfucker! Let's go outside! Me and you! I'll rip your leg off and beat you over the head with it!"

And that is John's sister talking.

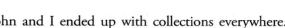

John and I ended up with collections everywhere. I mean *everywhere*. I felt like I was suffocating in collections. We had knick-knacks and whatnots all over the house. The girls were told never to touch them. They were valuable collections.

I'd stand in my kitchen and stare at round glass eggs that had scary faces painted on the front. I'd look the other way and be face-to-face with these little babies sitting on a shelf with ceramic heads and cloth bodies. I couldn't escape. I'd walk into the bedroom and the thimble collection was prominently displayed on a shelf as if we were honoring the thimbles in some way.

Slowly, over months, I began boxing the collections so they wouldn't get broken. Yes, that's why I boxed them. For their own safety. This angered people: "If you aren't going to display the wooden pig collection, why the fuck did you not let us display it at our house? Fuck John's wife."

I think a collection should have meaning. I have a magazine and newspaper collection. I collect magazines with amazing covers of events that changed the world. Like September eleventh. Afghanistan. Iraq. The hurricanes in New Orleans.

I'm not saying, Oh, look how smart I am, I have a better collection. But I am saying, I have a better collection because it makes sense. That's all. One day, I'll be able to show my grandchildren history. I'm not saying that a glass egg collection isn't relevant. I'm saying, Who exactly is it relevant to? And if that person is you, okay, but what's wrong with you?

John's family has become my family over the course of twenty years, and I can call on them for anything.

We spend holidays and birthdays and special occasions together. I love them. But a baby head collection?

I thought John was the worst person in the world to watch television with because he clicks and clicks and clicks. But then the twin brother moved in. Have you ever known someone who looked completely normal, but they started talking and you realized something was terribly wrong? Like some of the neurotransmitters in the brain are not quite connected? That's Geo.

> *I'm watching a show that has been on for forty-five minutes. Geo walks in, sits down and says, "Who's that? Are they married? Why are they in that building? Whose kid is that?"*
>
> *Or I'm watching a movie and he sits down and says, "Did I tell you about what happened when I was going to the store? I was driving and this car cut me off."*
>
> *I continue watching my movie.*
>
> *He says, "He almost hit me. Missed me by an inch."*
>
> *I nod and then turn back to the television.*
>
> *"Did you know that I was in the marching band when I was in middle school? I played the trumpet."*

I still have no response.

"Did you know that I cleaned my room today?"

No response.

He says, "Where's John?"

"In the garage."

"What is he doing?"

"Testing his weed blower."

"Really?" There's a pause while he mulls over that bit of information. "I may have to check that out."

"Really? Because I never get tired of hearing you talk."

Minutes later I hear screaming from the garage. I look out the window and see the fifty-year-old twins with masks on, howling with laughter, dramatically stumbling around with the weed blower blowing crap all over the yard.

I watch for a minute, but then I hear Mom ringing her bell. Someone kill me.

I try to do different things each holiday. I'm trying to create a tradition, but I'm the only person who ever gets excited about these projects.

Last year I gave the whole family a project. I asked every person to write one page about each family member. About why they love them, why they appreciate them, maybe a funny memory. The plan was to gather the pages a few days before Christmas and put each family member's pages together in a nice little binder with their name on the front. I gave them all thirty days.

I wrote my pages, and Jen wrote her pages even though she had pneumonia. And you know the only other person who finished the project? Mom. Granted, you couldn't read what she wrote because of the Parkinson's. But she put in the effort. I did read something about the birth of our Lord and Savior Jesus Christ. I also could make out the words "manger" and "camel" and "virgin."

This year, Christmas is canceled, but what I'm doing is something I've never done before. Every time I pass one of those people ringing the bell outside the store, I put what I can in the bucket.

I also try once a week to buy some cans for the food drive. Why haven't I done this before? Because I was consumed with spending every dime I had so the kids would love me. Coach purses, cell phones, Guess sunglasses, Gucci such and such.

I wonder if people a long time ago felt about Christmas the way we do now. I wonder if Mary and Joseph saw the three wise men walk up with the gifts and said, "Oh, great. Now we gotta get them something."

I can't cook and I don't want to learn. John didn't marry me for my skills in the kitchen. He married me because of my dazzling personality. I say, "Do you want a Hungry Man frozen meal, or can we just do something simple?"

People don't realize that some of the frozen entrées require more effort than others. Some, you just poke with a fork. Others, you have to peel back, and stir, and then put them back in. Some days I simply don't have that kind of energy or time to be pulling back and poking and stirring.

Food is not something I feel passionate about, so I don't prepare food in my house for my family to enjoy. I am merely trying to keep them alive.

Here's another thing that I have simply made a decision about: I'm done learning. It's a personal choice. I don't want to learn another thing. I want to take all the information in my head and just run out the rest of my life with that information.

I guess some would say it depends on what you have in there already. I don't have much, but I have enough. If someone says, "Did you know…" I stop them and say, "No, I didn't know, but don't tell me." I want to spend the rest of my life saying, "I have no idea."

In fact, there are some things in my brain right now I can do without knowing. But I can't erase them out of my head. I have an overwhelming amount of drug information in my head. Do I need it? No. But it's there. Just in case I have to scream at a health insurance company. Otherwise, I don't use it. It sits on the back burner of my brain waiting to pounce on some unsuspecting caseworker.

I know everything I need to know. I can still read the speed limit signs. I know my PIN for the ATM. I just don't want any more information.

I needed to get my hair done, but I didn't have any money. My husband suggested that I go to the place where he gets his hair cut for twelve dollars. He said, "How can you go wrong for twelve dollars?"

Well, a woman can go *very* wrong for twelve dollars. A twelve-dollar haircut could ruin your life and change your gender. A woman can't even tip a hairdresser for twelve dollars.

The last time I paid under fifty dollars for a haircut, I walked out with a mullet. A bad mullet.

You say, "A 'bad mullet' is an oxymoron"? Here's how to tell a good mullet from a bad one. If you have a good mullet, you should look like one person from the front, and then when you turn around, you look like a completely different person. If someone looks at you and they can tell you have a mullet by looking at the chopped front and sides of your hair, that is a bad mullet. In other words, you need to chop far enough back to make the mullet kick ass. Trust me, I grew up in a trailer. I know a sweet mullet when I see one. And if you're a woman and you accidentally get a mullet, whatever you do, do not wear a fanny pack or play tennis during that time. You will attract a gal pal.

I end up cutting my hair myself in my bathroom. I cut my bangs, and I accidentally cut them too short. I look exactly like my fourth grade picture. The day before picture day, my mother said, "Tomorrow is picture day, so come sit still and I'll cut your bangs so everyone can see your face."

Every woman in the world has that one school picture with the bangs that are half an inch long. The picture is all forehead with uneven bangs that look like they were cut with a cheese grater.

My hair is destroyed, so I have no choice but to deal with my bushman eyebrows because I have no hair to cover them. I get the electric trimmer that I always use, and I look away just for one second and shave most of one eyebrow off.

I come out of the bathroom and John says, "Oh! So you cut your hair." He doesn't say, it looks good, or it looks nice, he just says, "So you cut your hair." Then he says not to worry it will grow back.

I have to get out of the house. I have forty-six cents in my purse, but I need to get out. I go for a walk at an outdoor mall, and on the sidewalk there is the boys' choir singing their Christmas songs. Everyone is watching and smiling and singing along. They're all so excited about the holiday.

I'm just standing there looking at them thinking what I always think when I see a boys' choir, which is, Who dressed them? What minivan-driving mother picked these humiliating cruise ship shorts and sweater vests? Really? And here I am, mullet expert, now the judge of queer seven-year-olds, watching their chemically unbalanced mothers. The women are wearing sweatshirts that say things like, "Happy Birthday, Jesus!" They beam with pride while watching their boys. Meanwhile, my shaved eyebrow makes me look like I have a surprised expression on my face, which I don't.

I walk away and go into the makeup and hair product store, Ulta. All I can see is fifty women talking to themselves with their Janet Jackson headsets, which are channeled into their cell phones. All fifty of them have the popular white-tipped nails, hair highlights, hair extensions, and teeth so white that it's like looking into the sun if they smile at you.

The good news is that most of them don't smile. I overhear their phone conversations: "Last Christmas, that mother fucking piece of shit gave my daughter a six dollar Barbie, but we spent over two hundred fucking dollars on his kids that are the god-damn spawns of Satan."

I feel like the Hunchback of Notre Dame and back out the door. I go to PetSmart where I won't be judged. Then I go to the bookstore where I am always welcome because I blend. Even with my one eyebrow. Everyone blends in at the bookstore. I love the bookstore. The smell, the music, all the books.

I'm looking at all the bestsellers and thinking about my book. I read the back of a few of the books about the authors. Every one of them says something like, "Carol lives in the Rocky Mountains with her husband, Jeff, and their two cats, Salt and Pepa." Or,

"Dave lives in the Vermont wilderness with his wife, Madge, and their dog, Mr. Bossy."

I think to myself, I wish I was a real writer. I wish my computer looked out on snow-covered trees in the middle of the woods. I wish I could look out that window and drink some herbal tea and people wouldn't disturb me because I'm "working." I'd be in a room filled with books and dark wood floors, my long-haired dog lying on the beautiful rug I got in Japan, a few feet away from the gentle flames of the fireplace. Sip, sip.

My dad was one of the original starving artists. One day, when we were already living like refugees, Dad walked in the house and said, "I quit my job. I'm going to write a book. We're going to see some hard times but I need you guys to support me on this."

What? I didn't know people did things like this. Even *with* his income, we were eating rice three times a day. Half the time we didn't have electricity or water. We're going to see some hard times? What? No rice? Really?

He sat in his pajamas for about two months writing his book. I was a twenty-something waitress and single mom, living with my parents, plus Jen and April. My grandfather, who had Parkinson's Disease, lived with us, and my brother, Patrick, was in high school. My brother, Mark, and his wife lived there for a little bit, too. My sister, Lisa, and her two kids, Michael and Ashley, also lived there for a while. It was a full boat and now we were going to see some hard times?

We all had our various jobs, and we would walk past Dad every day as he sat in his pajamas writing his book. It didn't matter how starving we were or what utilities they turned off, he wouldn't budge. He was not going to get a job until his book was complete.

Thank God he thought his book was finished two months later.

I tell people about my dad because now I'm writing a book, and I feel like I've been writing it since I was a fetus. I've rewritten it seventy-five times. I've read it a gazillion times. And there is no light at the end of the tunnel. But Dad completed his book in two months, God bless America! Back to work! Go buy some rice!

I am not a starving artist. Well, at least we aren't starving *because* I'm an artist. I have always worked as I pursued whatever dream I've had. It's because of my father. Watching him follow his dreams while the walls fell down around him was painful. That's not something I will ever do. I work, I buy the rice, I cook the rice. If we need more rice, I make more money.

At the end of the day when all of what I feel are my responsibilities are taken care of, I write. I have waited my entire life to be able to just sit and write my book, and I've realized that day will never come. So I have to accept the idea that if I am going to write a book, I have to do it while I take care of my life. It may take longer, but it will eventually get written.

Dreams. Dreams are great. But buy shoes for the baby before you join the band. You want to be a supermodel? Do your best runway walk into the community college. Put your long thin legs under the desk and open a book, just in case. You have wanted to open a sausage store your whole life? Get a job in a sausage store so you can see the inner workings of the sausage industry. You're an actor? Clock in and "act" like you're a checker in a grocery store.

I'm not down on dreams. I think dreams are really fun. But dreams can be really *unfun* if you are living on the sidewalk and dumpster diving for your lunch. I'm not anti-dreams. I'm pro-electricity.

———— ❦ ————

This book was originally what people would call a "memoir." But because I'm a stand-up comic, it became something else. It's a book about true things that have happened, written by a comic—and everyone knows comics are completely full of shit.

As a comic, you have a concept in your head of something that is funny. You take that funny thing, and you bend it and twist it and you go down every different path. Much of what is written in this book is me, doing that. Woven into that are the things in my life that have almost broken me as I walked down the road. So this book is an exact replica of my life. The events exactly the way they unfolded. The truth. Plus the funniest thing I can think of to help me survive the truth. I'm confident that people are bright enough to differentiate between me being funny and me telling the truth. Because in this book, it's both.

I'm a checker in a grocery store. But when I put Mom to bed, and Moses too if he's here, and John falls asleep, and Carly is locked up in her room doing Jesus Christ God knows what, then, I am a writer. I wait until the next day is over and do the same thing. Type, erase, type, erase, ambulance, sip, sip. When my book comes out and they write about the author it's going to say:

Dina is the Maya Angelou of grocery store checkers. She lives in Phoenix with her husband, John, and her mother who has Parkinson's Disease, and her grandson, Moses, who has cerebral palsy, and his mom, April, who has a drug-crazed boyfriend who wants to burn Dina's house down, and a daughter named Jen who is a complete lesbian, and another daughter, Carly, who is a heroin addict. And they all have a dog named Squirt who is struggling with her weight.

Divine Order

I am dreaming. I am sitting in the middle of the ocean in a tiny boat with no paddles. I can feel the roll of the water under the little boat, and it is quiet except for small splashes of water every now and then. I don't know how I got here, in a boat, with no paddles in the middle of the ocean. I'm just sitting here. I can't see land in any direction, but I'm not afraid. I am calm. At complete peace. Just sitting in a tiny boat in the middle of the ocean.

———❈———

The earliest memory I have is me, sitting on a curb in my Girl Scout uniform, waiting for my dad to come out of a bar. He told my mom he was taking me somewhere. And he did. To sit on the curb in front of a bar on a slimy street in Albuquerque.

Every hour or so he would peek his head out and say, "You okay?"

Sure, Dad. Couldn't be better.

Then he'd go back in the bar.

Periodically, I'd also lift my head to say, "No sir. I don't have any spare change. I'm seven."

I remember getting home and my mom and dad had a scene

on the front lawn. Just a screaming thing, but I guess I was supposed to get one of my Girl Scout awards for making sugar cookies into shapes with a screwdriver. It was a pretty big deal and I missed it. I look back now and realize that was the last award of any kind that was offered in my direction. Today, I wish I had it because like I said, that was it. I don't have one single award to show for any great deed in my life. That Sugar Cookie Award was my last shot at greatness. And Dad blew it for me. It didn't matter to me that all the girls were getting the same award.

I don't get the concept of giving an award to everyone. Other than the Sugar Cookie Award, when I was a kid we had winners and we had losers. Period. Sometimes you won. Sometimes you lost.

Mentally handling "winning" was easy. You smiled and coasted through your sweet life until the next challenge. If you were deemed a "loser," your brain went into automatic wait-until-we-meet-again-I-will-annihilate-you-if-it-kills-me mode. It's called competition and it is something we face every single day of our lives.

When I was in the ninth grade, I was a gymnast. There was another girl on the team named Andrea. We were in constant competition to beat each other. I could not miss one day of school because Andrea might learn a great stunt while I was out. One day Andrea said to me, "Your socks are inside out." This provoked me into channeling Nadia Comaneci and becoming the greatest gymnast that cafeteria had ever seen.

Not too long after that, I dropped out of school and was pregnant with my first child, which is another story. But who really won? Andrea? I think she went on to college and got a law degree. Big deal, Andrea. Your Vera Wang skirt is inside out.

My point is you cannot function in the world without knowing how to respond to losing. It's the same as hearing the word "no." It's every day of our lives. It's a part of our lives. It is life.

A sports guy said, and I quote, "Show me a good loser and I'll show you a loser." You know who had this attitude? Nadia Comaneci. All the greats. Michael Phelps. Robert Downey, Jr. Bea Arthur. They all wanted to win. And they did! Michael Phelps didn't say, "I just have fun flipping around in the water in my Speedo." Are you kidding? He said, "I will win."

My dad got a medical release from the Navy because he climbed up a pole on a ship in the middle of the ocean and said he wouldn't come down until they discharged him. He finally fell off the pole because of leg cramps. They discharged him.

He was an alcoholic. He would walk over to the refrigerator, open the door and say, "I guess I'd better go get some milk." Then he'd leave and wouldn't come back for a couple of weeks.

Here's the comedy part of the story. He'd actually walk in, weeks later, with the gallon of milk.

He'd walk in the door carrying the milk and all five of us kids would think, Thanks, Dad. Now I can have that bowl of cereal I wanted two weeks ago.

He did stuff like this all the time. Once we had to go pick him up, two hours from where we lived, in a little tiny mining town at three in the morning because some bikers were holding him hostage until he paid his bar tab.

So my mom loaded all five of us in the green VW van to go save his life. She took all of us because we were too small to stay home alone. We got there in the middle of the night, Mom went in the little rundown bar and came out with Dad following her like a child. He got in the passenger side and looked back at all the children wrapped in blankets and said, "Wow! Am I glad to see you guys!"

When I was about nine, my siblings and I fell out of our moving van at an intersection. My dad didn't notice for about five blocks.

It was back before seat belts. It was also back before parents used any sort of common sense whatsoever. It was a time when you didn't raise your children. You just fed them and they got bigger.

My sister, Lisa, didn't really participate in dangerous activities, but my brothers and I could have been taken to the emergency room any given day. I was more boy than I was girl. I was a tiny, stick-skinny, messy-haired, dirty-faced six-year-old, and I said the fuck word more than any other human being on the face of the earth.

I have no idea why I loved that word so much. I think it was because it got such a grand reaction. Adults' eyes would roll back in their heads and then they would tell me, "The language, Dina! My goodness! Is this how Jesus wants you to speak?"

I didn't think Jesus cared. I still don't. I think Jesus has bigger fish to fry. Like starving children all over the world. Like hatred and racism and murderers and rapists. Me saying the fuck word is not something Jesus is going to have time to address for a long, long time.

We lived on a couple acres of land with four other families. It was a religious community, but if you called it a commune, my parents would flip. It was more of a trailer park cul-de-sac blessed by God. When there was an injury, it was "given to God." If the person was not healed, we gave it to God again. And so on, until enough time passed that God either healed you or the wound closed by itself.

Among our favorite games were, "Lie in the street and jump up before a car runs you over." Which explains itself. Then there was "Pull us with the truck," where we would sit on a flattened box and be pulled through a field with a rope attached to a truck at fifty miles an hour. Also self explanatory—and fantastic fun for the people watching from the back of the truck.

We played several games that involved dangerous acts from the back of a truck. One hundred percent of the emergency room conversations included the word "truck."

Our all-time favorite game was sitting in the back of the truck while it moved down the street, grabbing branches from the trees hanging over the dirt road. If you were successful, you would dislocate your wrist or, even better, your whole arm. And if you really had some nuts, you'd hold on long enough to be physically ripped out of the back of the truck. With the people watching from the moving truck howling with laughter as you hit the dirt road. If you could break a few ribs, you could bring all the people in the truck to their feet, which of course was the goal.

My sweet grandson, Moses, is eight. I cannot imagine him riding in the back of a truck. Are you fucking kidding with me? And on top of that watching him standing up in the back of the moving truck grabbing branches from the trees? Holy Jesus, it isn't going to happen. What the hell were my parents talking about in the front of the truck that enabled them to ignore the fact that one of their kids was about to rip a limb off? My grandson is lucky if I let him sleep without a helmet.

My dad is driving around the corner and all five of us kids, including my little brother, are trying to stand up in the back of the van without touching anything. We are actually small enough to stand straight up. He turns too fast at a busy intersection, the first kid bumps the door open, and there you have it. Young children lying all over the busy street.

Dad drives on for a while before he notices that he is missing a van full of children. He comes back to get us, and other people are already helping us.

He skids the green van into the intersection and jumps out saying, "They're mine! I got it!" One kid at a time, he lays us in a pile in the back of the van, and drives away. We lay back there, completely injured, moaning. A giant pile of busted up children. He takes us home and "calls out" all the religious people who live on the religious land. My mother is at the laundry mat.

All the anointed people congregate into the bedroom where my father has laid us on beds. All five of us are bleeding and in shock, so they begin the "laying on of hands." Very loudly. Almost screaming. It is desperate praying. Suddenly, my mother walks in.

Dad tells her what happened and she loses it. She starts screaming that we need to go to the hospital. Some of the loud praying people explain that the color is coming back to our faces and maybe they should keep going with the prayer. Mom starts screaming and threatening people to carry us to the fun van and take us to the hospital before she strangles every "Goddamn person in the room." We go to the hospital.

That was the last time we played "Fucking around in the van." That's when we started playing "Throw things up on the electrical wires on the street and see what we can hang up there."

Once my brother, Mark, hooked a bike handle on the electric wire. The electricity in the whole neighborhood went off for about two days. He was a legend after that.

I believe in God. I also believe in miracles. But I also believe that God made certain people to be intelligent enough to be doctors. Doctors help you when you've fallen out of a van. At the hospital my parents were still going back and forth about which treatment works best. The hospital and doctors or the loud desperate praying. I think doctors and prayer work hand-in-hand.

Growing up, we lived in a trailer on the Land Blessed by God. At one time, we lived in a little house on the Land Blessed by God, but that house was condemned by the city. I guess if God blesses the house, but the city condemns it, the city wins.

The trailer we moved into wasn't a sweet double-wide with a pretty flower box out front. It was a single wide, with wooden steps, parked on a huge lot of dirt. It was so small that if someone was walking down the hallway, you had to wait until the other person passed because both of you couldn't fit. Fistfights were common. If you started down the hallway and one of my brothers wanted through, you backed out or he would back you out.

We spent many days without electricity which was great because we could play outside under the street lights while my parents sat on the wooden steps of the trailer. My dad smoking cigarettes and my mom thanking God for everything.

When my father worked, he was a school teacher, so he was

off on weekends. All five of us were small, but we would wait anxiously for his call every weekend morning. Dad would yell from his bed, "I wish I had a friend!" That meant he wanted one of the kids to bring him a cup of coffee.

All five of us would rush to the kitchen and try to be the first to get the cup of coffee. The winner got to walk down the narrow hall in the trailer with hot coffee being splashed on his or her arms by the losers who were following too close behind. Each of us five kids wanted to be the winner because even though it meant first degree burns on your arms, it also meant you got to be Dad's friend. You'd hand Dad his half a cup of coffee, and he'd smile at you like you had accomplished something really amazing. My mom would also smile, and we all knew it was because when the alcoholic is smiling, we may have a shot at a half-decent day.

We were raised in Albuquerque, New Mexico. Now that I live in Phoenix, I remember the sweet things about Albuquerque. Like chili. Red or green, we ate it every meal when I was growing up. People roasted green chili on the side of the street in Albuquerque. We could smell it when we rolled the window down. It was the most amazing smell ever. We wanted to pull over and buy some, but typically we had a freezer full. We put green chili on everything–on eggs in the morning, on a burger at lunch, and with beans and fried potatoes for dinner.

The only place to get Hatch green chili is Hatch, New Mexico. Miles and miles of green chili growing along the side of the road. Unless it's a particularly hot batch of Hatch green chili, it's not the heat of the chili that makes it amazing. It's the taste. Hatch chili has a very distinctive, hot-sweet flavor. People who grew up in Albuquerque can tell the difference between Hatch chili and a chili that was just aspiring to be a Hatch chili.

Once, my grocery store had a guy out front with a sign saying he was roasting Hatch green chili. I asked my boss if it was actually Hatch green chili. My boss says, "Yeah! Hatch chili! Well, it's from California." You can only get Hatch chili from Hatch.

After growing up eating chili all day, we moved to Phoenix, walked in to a Mexican restaurant and the waiter said, "Red or green sauce?" Sauce? Is it chili or is it sauce? The waiter said, "It's chili sauce." Oh, God. Toto, we are not in Albuquerque anymore.

If you say "red sauce" in Phoenix, they always bring out the same sauce at every Mexican restaurant. The dark, dark red, weird…sauce.

Red chili in New Mexico is a beautiful color of red with an orangey tint. It's a magical color of red. When we go in a new restaurant and I see a waitress walk by and the red sauce is that deep, dark red, I order tacos. I've eaten many a taco since we've lived in Phoenix.

The food, oh God, the food in Albuquerque is ridiculously awesome. When I go back to visit my sister, I force her to eat Mexican food all day. I never get tired of it. And it's not two or three places. It's ten amazing Mexican restaurants on every single street—little places that were once individual houses are now restaurants with ten tables and lines out the front door.

Also in Albuquerque, people don't paint their front doors bright blue because it's stylish. They paint them bright blue because in New Mexico that's the color a door is supposed to be. Bright blue, bright green, or orange. Wooden wagon wheels lying around because they belonged to someone at some point. Amazing little houses with flat roofs, mud walls, and red trim.

The smells…the flavors…the culture…Albuquerque had it. But it also had snow, which is not my cup of tea. I cannot stand to be cold. In Phoenix, if it dips under 70, I complain until March when it goes back up to 95. Or until June when it's 115 like it should be.

My parents had eight kids, including twins who died at birth. My brother, Patrick, was born when the five older kids were all at least ten or eleven. He was the cutest child ever. He was spoiled by all the older siblings and my parents. As spoiled as a kid can be living in squalor.

I wonder how my parents and other parents did it with so many children. How do you feed them, or provide them with clothing?

I hated going to the grocery store with my mom. First, she paid with food stamps. That humiliated me. And if that wasn't bad enough, she would never have enough food stamps. She'd have to put things back. She'd say, "Take this off. Now how much?" And she'd keep doing this until she had enough food stamps. During all this I'd wait in the car. Now that I'm sort of grown up, I'm sure the food stamps embarrassed her more than they embarrassed me.

Mom and I would go to the laundry mat, but by the time we could afford it, we had fifteen loads of clothes. We walked in the laundry mat carrying enormous bundles of clothes wrapped in bed sheets and take up half the washers. All the other people stared angrily at us. The three-load laundry people always judge.

One Christmas we all got bikes. I still have no idea how my parents financed five bikes. But my dad spent all night Christmas Eve putting the bikes together. I woke up in the middle of the night because I had a really high fever. I walked into the living room, and my dad was sitting on the floor with half-assembled bikes everywhere. I heard him say, "Son of a goddamn bitch," as he was working on a bike. I was so sick I couldn't even connect that we were getting bikes for Christmas. My mom rushed me back to my room.

The next morning, surprise! Santa Claus brought us bikes! I was still sick and could hardly get out of bed for the unveiling of the bikes.

My brothers and sister are out like lightning the second the sun comes out on Christmas morning. They all take off on their new bikes and don't come back for hours. But I'm sick, so my parents won't let me go out in the 10 degree weather to take a spin on my pink bike with the pink basket. Instead, I sit with my fever on my bed crying.

After more than an hour of dramatic crying on my part, my parents say I can ride my bike once around the block. So I get on my bike and ride once around the block with the bitter wind hitting my face and snot dripping down my nose. I bring my bike in and park it next to my bed and fall asleep for the rest of the day. Merry Christmas.

I loved my bike. I was nine. I spent most of my time pretending I was making commercials for my bike. Here was how the commercial went: I rode my bike out to the middle of this desolate land and parked it. I dramatically looked at my bike and pretended I was crying. Then I kissed the handlebar and slowly walked away with my head hung down. I walked about ten steps, then I turned and looked at my bike, then ran back and hugged it. Then, in my head the commercial guy said, "Pink bike. The bike you can't abandon." At the time, this made sense.

I spent a lot of time pretending. I played Jeannie C. Riley really loud and sang "Harper Valley PTA." I was also the star of "Grease" in my room. I sang with a hairbrush and danced.

Sometimes all of us kids were a singing group. We were the Jackson Five except white with white stringy hair. The albino Jackson Five. We danced and sang "One Bad Apple" while we took turns flipping on and off the lights to make it more concert-like.

We also had to take turns being Michael. I felt I was the best Michael of all of us because I had the moves. I could get my freak on at a very young age. My siblings, on the other hand, were just as white as white can be. It was sad to watch.

Out of six children, five of us became alcoholics or addicts or both, so we really did have the makings to be the next Jackson Five. But only if we had just put my sister, Lisa, way in the back so you couldn't see her dance like the whitest person in the world. Lisa can sing like an angel, but she is hands down the worst dancer I have ever seen.

I began making pretend commercials as far back as I can remember. They weren't all as good as the pink bike commercial, but I thought they were television-worthy. Actually the only other commercial I remember, I created before the pink bike commercial.

It was another time when I was really sick, this time with the stomach flu, and my mom would always give us 7 Up when we had the stomach flu. I pleaded with my mother to let me have a Coca-Cola. After listening to me beg, she went to the store and got some Coke. I drank the cold Coke with my fever and that's when the commercial came to me.

The commercial started with me holding my head down and holding my stomach. Looking very sick. Then I dramatically look on my table and there sits a beautiful cold Coke. Then I take a drink of the Coke and hold it up with my arm outstretched and the commercial guy says, "Coke! It's the best drink in the fucking world!" So you can see from a young age I had a natural gift for advertising.

One place we lived in when I was young was a tiny house with random rooms built onto the house to make it bigger. You think that's a closet? Wrong. It's a room. You think you're going outside? Wrong. Another room.

But as the other rooms were added, they didn't add heat so the living room was the only room in the whole house that had heat. It was a big heater that was level to the floor that blew hot air out into the room.

In Albuquerque, the winters can get really cold. Lots of snow and wind. You need heat. So all five of us older kids would pray we would be the first up in the morning so we could lie in front of that blowing heat. Mainly because we were frozen solid by the time the sun came up. I'd open my eyes, jump up and run to the living room. There was nothing more devastating than running around that corner and realizing that someone had already assumed the position in front of the heat. There they'd be, lying sound asleep on the floor with the warm air blowing on them.

So I would stand there and look at them. I was cold. I needed to get warm. I knew the keys to the kingdom were going to come in the form of spooning with my sibling.

Spooning with a brother doesn't just happen as naturally as you'd think. I knew the second I touched his back he'd punch me in the side of the head. But it was so worth it to stop my teeth from chattering. The best I could do was lie next to him and at least warm my back.

We would fight about the heat. We tried taking turns but that didn't work. So I'd have to loiter around the living room so the second the heat hog got warm enough, I could rush into position. It was like heaven lying there on that filthy floor, warm and happy.

My brother, Mark, was a really great basketball player at our school. He made the team, and then my dad used Mark's basketball shoe money to pay Dad's bar tab. So Mark got pissed off. He went into a sporting goods store, put on the most expensive pair of gym shoes, and walked out the door.

The problem was he couldn't walk around in the stolen shoes because Mom and Dad would notice if someone was wearing shoes that were more expensive than all the furnishings in our entire house. So Mark put the shoes on in his room. You could stand by the door and hear him: "He shoots! He scores!"

He'd come out of his room really sweaty, and Mom would say, "Why are you so sweaty and red faced?" Mark would shrug his shoulders.

Every time Mom and Dad left, Mark put the tennis shoes on and ran through the house. We all sat on the couch in our shoes wrapped in silver duct tape and watched Mark run back and forth: "He shoots! He scores!" Mom and Dad pulled up, Mark ran to his room, and we all laughed. It made us proud to be related to someone with such nice shoes.

When my parents found the shoes under Mark's bed, they took Mark to the store and made him confess. Mark promised never again to steal shoes that he desperately needed. The store manager accepted the apology and agreed to take back the shoes—until he saw that they were already worn out. So the manager told my dad he had to buy the shoes. My dad didn't have any money because, well, beer. So Dad said, "How much are they?" The guy told him. My dad said, "I don't want to pay for the store. Just the shoes." Dad wrote the guy a check.

The rest of us were waiting at home wondering if Mark was going to prison. No, he wasn't. He ran in the front door wearing the shoes and acted like he was making a basket: "He shoots! He scores!"

So Dad wrote the check and the next two months we didn't have water or electricity. And you could say it was because of the shoes, but really it was because of the bar tab.

My sister, Lisa, was the beauty queen in our house, and she got straight A's. She also won awards weekly. I couldn't get one fucking sugar cookie award, and there she was setting another award on the milk crate covered with a towel. "Oh, don't put your drink there! That's where I put my awards!"

I was average-looking and got solid D's. Which didn't matter to me since my dad didn't really notice. I could not impress my dad if I shot solid gold bricks out of my ass.

I see Dad sitting on the wooden steps in front of the trailer smoking a cigarette. Suddenly I feel like this is the time to really impress him.

I decide I'm going to do a round off right there on the dirt road. I start running, I pick up speed, anticipating how thrilled he will be that I'm his daughter. I'm at top speed and I see out of the corner of my eye that he's standing and walking in the door of the trailer. Holy shit! I've got to do this now! But I lose my footing and only do half the round off, which is the equivalent of diving directly into the dirt. All I do is scrape up my arms and legs and make dirt fly up all around me.

I look up and see Dad peek his head out of the screen door. He yells, "What the heck are you doing?! You're gonna kill your-self! My, God, get in this house."

I limp to the trailer as Lisa comes down the road in some boy's car. Her long beautiful hair blowing in the wind, and in her outstretched arm is what looks like an Emmy.

I have been phobic as far back as I can remember. You know that cartoon where Wiley Coyote is standing on top of a speeding train and the train goes into a tunnel? He forgets to duck and his outline is smashed into the concrete arch above the tunnel. As a child I would wonder, What if I am standing on a train and I don't duck fast enough to go through the tunnel? This was some-thing I actually worried about.

I'm afraid of everything. I trace it back to the second grade. My second grade class went on a field trip. We were all sitting on the grass in a big circle somewhere, drinking lemonade. I took a big gulp from my straw, and I swallowed two or three seeds. I said to the little girl sitting next to me, "I just swallowed some lemon seeds."

She looked at me and said, "You're going to grow a lemon tree in your belly."

I thought, Oh my God! A lemon tree in my belly! Someone help me!

I spent the rest of the field trip thinking about the lemon tree growing in my belly. How fast will it grow? Will the branches poke out of my skin? Could I trim the branches so I could wear regular clothes? Would the lemons be edible? Would my parents be embarrassed by my condition, yet pleased because my lemons are so tasty?

By the time I got home from the field trip, I was in complete panic. I ran to my mother, grabbed her shirt, and said, "I swallowed some lemon seeds!"

She continued doing whatever she was doing.

I got more desperate. "Mom! I swallowed some lemon seeds! A girl said I am going to grow a lemon tree in my belly!"

In my entire life there has been one time I needed my mother to be sure of something and this was the time. I needed her to be firm and confident and absolute. Instead, she looked down at me with a smile and said, "Oh. I don't think so, Honey."

I don't think so? Good God in heaven, I might be growing a lemon tree in my belly. You don't think so. But you can't be sure? I sort of need you to be sure about this. I needed something to the effect of, "That is the silliest thing I have ever heard! Of course you will not grow a lemon tree in your belly!" But no. She didn't think it would happen.

I lay flat on my bed with my hand on my stomach waiting for some activity. Some movement. The scent of lemons. Something.

Weeks went by and there were no indications of any foliage growing in my stomach. But for months, any stomach ache was clearly from the lemon tree.

The rest of the second grade, I avoided the girl who informed me of the lemon tree in my belly. I felt she knew something the others didn't. Some sort of voodoo.

By the third grade, I began to believe I had food poisoning from dented cans. And off I went from there. Fear of flying. Fear of driving. Fear of all sorts of things. But it all started with the lemon tree.

Today, my favorite drink in the world is the Lemon Lime Slush from Sonic. I drink one every day, and most days I swallow a few seeds. I feel no fear. I only enjoy the deliciousness of my beautiful drink. Until it dawns on me that one of the workers could be disgruntled and may have put poison in my slush. Or my car could suddenly ignite into flames. Or I could be carjacked. Which could lead to chest pains.

I decided in the ninth grade that I had enough of an education to live out my life. But the law was that I had to complete ninth grade before I could quit school and start my great life.

So I had to pass each class with at least a D. In five classes, I had D's. But in biology, I had an F. I talked to my teacher and he said, "You'll never graduate anyway." Then he gave me a project that would give me the D. I had to collect fifty bugs, put them on a poster board and name each bug. So I waited until the day before to start the project, of course. I called friends over, and we walked all the fields and dirt roads and ditches until we found fifty bugs. We pinned each bug to the board and named them, sometimes making up names. I got on the bus that morning with my giant poster board with bugs pinned on it. Some people on the bus noticed that one of the bugs was still alive and spinning on the pin in circles.

I got to the school excited about getting the D. I remembered what my teacher had said about me never being able to graduate. It was graduation day for the seniors, so I borrowed a cap and gown from a friend.

I walked into the science room with my cap and gown, smiling, and handed the teacher my bug collection.

He looked at it and smiled and said, "Okay. I'll give you the D."

I smiled and said, "So I graduated after all."

He said, "If that's the way you want it."

I smiled and walked out, returned the cap and gown, and walked off the school campus with all my ninth grade knowledge. It seemed like a good idea at the time.

During my last year of school, I skipped lunch simply because of the trauma of the lunch process.

I think I was popular in school. I hung out with the popular people, went to the popular people's homes, and did things that only popular people did—like have the popular people pick me up for school in their pretty Mustangs. We'd get in the parking lot and turn the stereo up really loud just to show how fantastic we were. Of course it wasn't my sweet car, but who gives a shit? I'm riding shotgun.

There was a difference between me and them. They lived in big houses. I lived in a trailer. I was poor, but I was funny and had feathered hair like Farrah Fawcett, and that was just enough to get me in.

At lunch, there were three lunch lines. I seriously still can't believe this was their process. They had the "full-pay" line. This line was for the kids whose parents could afford to pay full price for the kid's lunch. Then there was the "reduced" line. These kids paid a reduced price for lunch. Then there was the "free" lunch line. That's the line I stood in. This was the line for kids who had parents who couldn't afford the forty cent hit for lunch—or the kids who were being raised by wolves.

We would walk into the cafeteria, being very popular, and then my entire group would break off from me and go to the full price line. I would walk over to the free lunch line.

Trying to maintain my popularity in the free lunch line was challenging. I had to make my group, the full-pay people, laugh from all the way across the cafeteria. It was my way of letting the people in the free lunch line know that I was actually with the popular full-pay people.

Sometimes I'd get my tray and sit down and the full-pay line was longer. So I'd sit by myself and push my food around and act like it didn't bother me sitting alone. My people would show up about the time I'd finish my lunch. It was worse when the free line moved slower than the full-pay. Then I'd get to the table and they would be already standing up to leave as I sat down. I would make some hysterical joke and walk out with them, dumping my food in the garbage. We'd walk around the school grounds just being cool and popular, but the blood would drain from my face because I was completely malnourished. Not Africa malnourished, but trailer-park malnourished.

Later, I decided to smoke cigarettes during lunch. I was still popular but not as much because I found the full-pay girls actually had sticks up their asses. So I found some better friends more suitable to my reality. My best friend's dad was in prison. She didn't have a car so we walked everywhere.

We would stand in front of the liquor store and give Indians money to buy us Boone's Farm wine. Staggering down the dirt road drunk, smoking cigarettes. Smoking, coughing, and laughing. Those were the days.

The highlight of the summer was going to the public pool. Back then, nobody had pools in their backyards. So the poor, rich and everyone in-between spent the weekends at the public pool. We looked forward to it all week.

It was the same process every public pool visit: find out who's there—hopefully the boy you are in love with—and look as sexy as you can even though you are thirteen. When you got there, you took off your outer clothing, thus unveiling the Greatest Show on Earth. Your one-piece suit that was too short for your long body, so it violently jammed up your money maker, reminding you not to dive into the pool because if you lifted your arms, hello paramedics.

That wasn't even the worst part of the greatest day of the week. The worst was the rubber swimming cap. This was invented by someone who hated girls. You took this tight—I mean tight—rubber cap and tried to get every strand of hair in the thing. As you did this, your eyes were watering because of the pain. When you finally got your hair in the cap and couldn't look more like an idiot, there were actual flaps that covered your ears. So if your friend said something to you, you had to lift your flap to hear her.

The cap was so tight that your eyes were stretched back into slits, and your mouth was also stretched, so it looked like you were smiling this serial killer grin that wasn't really a smile at all, but what could you do? Your hair couldn't be in the water because of the health code.

One summer I was able to get the "good" cap. The one with brightly colored rubber flowers that covered the entire surface of my round head. The ear flaps were giant rubber flowers. When I put this sweet cap on, with my one piece, I could feel the envy penetrating through the rubber. I would walk out of the shower room, cap on, five foot six, seventy pounds, and every boy at the pool fell madly in love with me. I'd be walking with my friend saying, "Is he looking over here?"

Then I'd lift my flap to hear her answer. Then flap back down on the ear. I was sure just the sight of me, gliding down that hot concrete with my flowered cap, was a treat for everybody.

It's been so many years since I stood in the free lunch line and wore that fabulous swim cap. Now I think about those days and it makes me happy. Riding in that yellow Mustang with the windows down. Listening to Earth, Wind and Fire, the wind blowing through my feathered hair creating that "hair shield" from the hairspray. Applying my lip gloss. The kind that made your lips look wet so when the wind blew, your hair stuck to your lips. I had it all going on. I was a pretty big deal. Then I quit school and got pregnant. That's what happens when you have Farrah Fawcett hair and lips like glass.

I was pregnant. We had a bunch of chickens in the backyard. My father had gone to some sort of religious conference, and a wild dog got in the chicken coop and almost killed the chickens.

So we got ahold of my dad and he said we had to butcher the chickens. The point of the chickens was to grow them up so we could kill them and eat them. We couldn't waste the chickens. So Dad told me, my mom, my sister, and my brother how to do it. First, you boil a pot of water on a fire in the backyard. Then you hammer two nails into a tree stump. Then you get an axe, lay the chicken's head in between the nails, look away and chop off the chicken's head. After that, you hold the chicken by the feet while it violently flaps around without its head, and then you dunk it in the boiling water, which makes all the chicken's feathers come off. Then you do a lot of cutting and scooping and gross crap and there you have it. Dinner.

I swear to God to this day, it's really stressful to eat chicken. My mom can hardly eat it at all, but the chickens had to be used. For food. I did not eat the chickens we murdered and I puked for days.

My grandmother died when she was 101. Her thing was Xanax. I was a teenager, and I didn't know how awesome and great Xanax was.

Grandma lived with us, and a couple of times a day she would scream in her angry voice, "Bring me my Xanax!!" Someone would quickly take it to her, and she would throw it in her mouth without water and just swallow it. Then she'd roll her wheelchair to the window and stare out for about ten minutes.

All it took was ten minutes, then she'd yell in a nice voice, "Dina! Come in here!" I'd go in her room and she'd say, "I'd like to sing you a song." She put her little Casio keyboard on her lap and started playing: "Take me out to the ballgame, take me out to the crowd, buy me some peanuts and Cracker Jacks, I don't care... (pause) Take me out to the ballgame..."

She knew one song and she only knew the beginning of it. I heard this song from Grandma a thousand times.

Something about the Xanax made her lipstick drip. Each morning she would dress up in these fantastic outfits—bright colors, matching perfectly, cheap jewelry everywhere and then red lipstick. Toward the late afternoon, after her second or third dose, she looked like a drunk clown.

She also acted like a drunk clown. One time she called me in, sang "Take Me Out to the Ballgame" again, and then she put the keyboard down and told me to come closer. She held my hands and said, "You know, your dad did get a little carried away with the liquor, but honey, you were a difficult child to raise." Then she picked up the keyboard: "Take me out to the ballgame..."

According to Grandma I was the reason my dad was drinking himself to death. She said, "But I love you anyway, Honey." Thanks, Grandma. I was a very powerful twelve-year-old. The interesting part is that I hadn't even begun to utilize my evil powers. I had only scratched the surface of ways to cause my father's constant drinking. Too bad my grandma died before she could see me burn the city down with the lasers that shot fire out of my eyes.

Grandma was in a wheelchair but it confused me. She didn't use the foot rests. I thought wheelchairs were for people who had limited movement in their legs. She would barrel through the house using her feet to push the chair forward. Like the Flintstones. She could move at a powerful pace. Her legs had giant muscles on them and she'd fly out of her room at about fifty miles an hour, completely wasted on Xanax and scream, "Is someone gonna make my biscuits?"

My grandma didn't walk an easy road. She came home from first grade one day, and her father had shot her mother and then shot himself. All of her siblings were shipped off to various places, but no one could take her because she was too young. So she was raised by nuns. She also outlived all three of her children. One, her only daughter, died at the age of sixteen.

So Grandma took shitloads of Xanax. Can you imagine being so old that you can take anything you want?! I can't wait for the day that I can scream, "Bring me my Xanax!"

"But Mom, you just had one."

"Go to hell! Bring me another one! My program is about to start!"

My mom's parents went to a Pentecostal church, and they were very strict. There was a lot of screaming in the church, and we were forced to sit through it if we stayed at their house. My grandfather was one of the main screamers.

They raised six children in a three-bedroom, six-hundred-square-foot house and lived there until they died. Literally. They died in the house.

When my siblings, our cousins and I slept at our grandparents' house, my grandfather said a long prayer at meal times. We kids did everything in our power to stifle our laughter. But we sat on a wooden bench, and we could feel the bench moving and know with our eyes closed that someone was laughing, which caused every child on the bench to laugh.

The last thing we wanted to do was laugh during the prayer because Grandpa punished us right there at the table. My grandfather was six foot four. When he walked in the house, he ducked through the door. If you were going to piss someone off, don't let it be him. And all it took was one slight giggle during the prayer.

We could feel it coming, and every person at the table was paralyzed with fear. Everything became slow motion. Grandpa raised his hand. His arm was long enough to reach a child sitting at the other end of the table. My grandmother put her fork down and crossed her hands and bowed her head. I'm pretty sure I remember hearing the *Jaws* soundtrack playing in the background. His hand, the size of a garbage can lid, would make its way across the table to the child who was not giggling anymore. Grandpa made an "O" with his middle finger and his thumb. His finger was the size of a giant bratwurst. Then he thumped the child on the head with that middle finger.

The unlucky recipient of the child abuse would have a headache for days. The pain was like your skull had been shattered. You could shake your head and hear loose things knocking around in there.

After the thumping everyone at the table sat in complete silence. Then Grandpa pointed his giant sausage finger in our faces and said, "You better get right with God." Despite our concussions, we'd mumble, "Okay." But then the very next time we sat down to eat, out of nerves, someone started laughing. Every single time. I think that's how we all ended up with brain damage.

My grandfather sat in his recliner every day for twenty years and fell asleep watching "As The World Turns." One day he fell asleep watching this show and never woke up. I bet that if he could have chosen how to die, that would have been the way.

Quietly watching his show. That's how I want to go. I want people to say, "She was watching *Keeping Up With the Kardashians*. And that was it."

My parents made all of us go to church when I was a teenager. My family sat at the front of the Catholic church we attended because we were the choir and house band. My father, sister, two brothers, and I played played the guitar and sang all the songs. We were like the Partridge Family except sometimes our dad was still drunk from the night before.

When my grandmother came to church, she would sing at the top of her lungs. It didn't matter where she was sitting, you could hear her over the entire congregation. I would be dying of embarrassment, but she felt like Dad was a celebrity sitting in the front of the church with his guitar. She wanted to show she was the lead singer's mother, and also show where he got his powerful vocal abilities from. She was with the band. I cringed when Grandma came to church because I knew I would be teased by my friends. "I sat in front of your grandmother. She popped my ear drum."

In this church I was crowned the troublemaker. My friends and I laughed during church. But the only person they could see laughing was me because I was sitting facing the entire congregation.

One time, we got caught stealing hosts—the little round wafers that Catholics served for communion. We went behind the school next door with an entire bag. They were delicious. We would say to each other, "The Body of Christ." And open our mouths for each other and then die laughing. Then we started shoving ten or twelve at a time in the other person's mouth, and we were choking and laughing rolling around on the concrete. We had almost eaten the whole bag when the priest came around the corner. Our parents were notified, and we were lectured about snacking on the Body of Christ.

There was also a white lace cloth at the church. It was a sacred cloth that went around to every Catholic church in the country. Each place had the sacred cloth for a week or so. It was sort of as if the white lace cloth was on tour.

My friend's parents were responsible for shipping it to the next location, so it was in a special box in the back seat of my friend's car. The box intrigued us, so we opened it and somehow the sacred cloth got ripped. We all thought we would be struck dead and sent immediately to hell because we ripped the sacred cloth that was expected in one piece at Sea World in San Diego. After telling our parents, we wished we had gone directly to hell. It was horrible. We had to confess our crime to the same priest who caught us savagely eating the Body of Christ just days earlier.

Around this time is when I met my first husband. He was trouble. Big trouble. The priest knew of him and cautioned my parents about our "relationship."

I go to confession, and it's the same priest with the hosts and the sacred cloth and the relationship advice.

The priest says, "Dina?"

I say, "Yes."

He tells me to come out of the booth. He tells me that he's been in the confessional all afternoon and it's hot in there, so he will hear my confession in the back room.

We get in the back room and he has a whole setup. A chair

and a sheet hanging down, and then a chair on the other side. So he says, "Much better."

So I start my confession. I start with all the generic sins... taking the Lord's name in vain, lying to my parents, eating the body of Christ. Then I confessed being one of the savages who tore the sacred cloth.

The sheet is thin. I can clearly see his outline behind it. He says, "Uh-huh. Okay. Anything else?"

I say, "No."

He says, "What about that boyfriend?"

"What do you mean?"

"I think you know what I mean. Do you have sex with this boy?"

I don't answer. He continues.

"What does this boy do to you? Does he touch you here or there? Does he do this or that?" But the priest is actually saying really graphic things.

I'm completely paralyzed with fear. I can see through the sheet that he is masturbating. I am trying to suck up my tears. I can see the door knob from where I'm sitting and I think if I can get to it before him, I can run out.

I sit there while he goes on like this for what seems like forever. Then I jump up, grab the door knob and run through the empty church screaming.

I get out the door and I am sobbing. My friend's mom has driven me to confession and asks me what happened. All I can get out is that I had to run out. She launches into the trouble I'm going to be in when she tells my parents.

I get home, and my friend's mom tells my parents that I ran out of confession and I was disrespectful to the priest. My parents

*don't even allow me one word. They march me to the car and
now we're driving back to the church where I am expected to
apologize to the priest for being disrespectful to him. I try to
explain and they won't let me talk. I'm a troublemaker.*

*The priest invites us into the rectory, and I can see a
glimpse of fear in his face. Until he finds out that I am there
to apologize to him for my disrespect while he was jacking off
in front of me. He sits there, smiling, waiting for his apology.
I'm crying. I apologize because I want out of there. He sweetly
smiles and says, "I forgive you." He looks like the devil. Afterwards, my parents are talking with him in the entryway. I look
on the coffee table and see his watch. I put it in my pocket. Fuck
him. When I get home I crush it with a hammer and throw it in
the ditch.*

After that I refused to go to church. I told my parents what happened, and they said I made the story up because I hated the
priest. They tried over and over to physically drag me out of the
house to go to church. I said I would never go back and I didn't.

After that I stopped believing in God.

Twelve years later, I was living in Phoenix. The phone rang
and it was my mother. She was crying. I thought, Oh my God,
what happened?

She said she picked up the morning paper, and right there on
the cover was the priest. They were taking him out of the rectory
in handcuffs. They were charging him with sexually assaulting
more than a hundred children. Many of the victims were kids I
went to church with. Mom was crying and saying how sorry she
was that she and my dad hadn't believed me. I told her I loved her,

and I was over it.

After I got off the phone with Mom, I began to think that it was this shit bag priest who I didn't believe in. And it was the whole idea of church in general that I didn't believe in. But did I actually believe in God? Because God was a separate idea. Could it be that this priest actually had stolen my belief in God, and that God had nothing to do with it? Was there really such a thing as God?

All I know is that my mom spent her entire life praying, and it seemed to me that her life sucked. Because that's the attraction to God, right? You pray for things and he gives you those things? If it is his "will"? Did God give my mom anything? Was it not in his will?

People talk about Divine Order. The people who are really pumped up about Divine Order are the people who have had a sweet Divine Order in their lives. I know that my life is what I have made it. But my mom?

Divine Order is the concept that every single thing in your day and your life is exactly how it is supposed to be.

Divine Order for some people is, "Went to college, got married, had three children who are now senators and oncologists, had seven grandchildren, then I died peacefully sitting on a blanket in the middle of my flower garden." That is a really nice Divine Order.

Then there are people with a different Divine Order. "Went to college, married an alcoholic, had six kids, twenty-four grandchildren, lived in my car, and died choking on a pretzel in the parking lot of a dollar store."

The Divine Order people are the same as the "money doesn't matter" people. The people who say "money doesn't matter" are the people with shitloads of money. If you ask an old lady who lives in the middle of a drug-infested, violent, poor community that she can't leave because she can't even afford bread, she might say that money matters. She might say that she had five children, but two of them were killed on the streets, and if she had money, she could have relocated herself and her children when they were small and maybe her life would look different today. So does money matter? Yes. It matters a lot. And was this her Divine Order? No. People got involved and fucked it up for her.

Because God is dealing with humans who are imperfect, the Divine Order can fall apart at any second. I'd like to think Divine Order is something to move toward. Sort of like a goal. I believe God has a plan for each one of us. I say, "Always try to move toward your Divine Order." Move toward the things in life that are good and kind and loving. And that may be the best we can do.

I've asked Mom about God more recently, and she says God has blessed her more than she can ever imagine. I look down at the hole in her sock and think, Really? She says she was blessed with "abundance."

Mom has this black pant suit. When she thinks of abundance, the pant suit is one of the things she uses as an example. She says she's still waiting for the right occasion to wear her pant suit.

Because of her medication, Mom obsesses about certain things. On the day I asked her about God, she talked about the black pant suit all day. At some point, she asked me to help her put it on.

I help Mom put on her black pant suit. She looks in the mirror.

"It still looks nice, right?" she asks.

The pant suit is solid black with shiny gold clasps. The gold clasps are enormous, and there are five or six that go down the front.

I say, "It really looks nice, Mom. I love it."

Then she says, "Where could I wear this?"

I say, "The Grammys?"

I change her out of the pant suit and guide her back to her chair. She spends the rest of the day mumbling and napping. I guess this is our Divine Order.

This is a letter of love a game of romance since 1810.
Copy this letter six times and give it to six friends.
No boys! This is not a joke! Then on the sixth day drink a
glass of milk and say the boy you like. Within six days he
will admit his love. If you break this chain you'll have bad
luck in love. It starts tomorrow!

Carly
nine years old

Chasing the Dragon

I am open to the idea of God, and Divine Order is jammed up my ass on a regular basis. This is the detailed version of my Divine Order, as I remember it.

Jennifer, my oldest daughter, was four-and-a-half years sober when she relapsed. Yes, the half year makes a difference. She was twenty-nine, an alcoholic, and an addict.

Coke, crack, heroin, meth, anything they were serving at the party, she would do it. Lots of it.

She was normal, and then it seemed like overnight, she began to disappear for days at a time. We would search and search for her, and then she'd walk in days later and not understand what the big deal was. She was with a friend and their phone didn't work. Why were we being so "dramatic"?

Soon after, she began showing signs of serious emotional problems. I have certain pictures in my head that never go away. One of them is from when Jen was about eighteen.

Jen is at our house to shower and eat before she goes back out on the road. The party road. She is taking a shower and I need something in the bathroom, so I walk in.

My daughter is standing there, naked. Her back is to me

and what I see almost makes me pass out. Cuts. Everywhere. Deep cuts. She has so many all across her back and arms.

I am so startled I quickly shut the door. I stand there for a moment holding the door handle. I am shaking and my heart is racing.

I open the door again and scream, "What the hell happened to your back?"

She says she slid down a hill and for me to get out.

I start crying and say, "You didn't slide down a fucking hill. Look at your back! Look at your arms! What are you doing? Why are you doing this?"

She quickly dresses, walks out of the house, and I don't hear from her for weeks. Then she calls and acts as if the whole event never happened. Then she moves to another state.

Jen was an alcoholic and now drugs were becoming a bigger part of her life. After she moved, she started using heroin. She was at a house party with people and they were all using heroin, so Jen joined in. She said years later that she first tried heroin because she was drunk. Now, years into our drug hell, I realize she probably said she was drunk so I would feel better.

One of the people at the party overdosed on the couch. So the people who lived in the house dragged this guy to the shower, closed the door, and left him there. He died in the shower. Someone's brother or son. He was lying dead in a shower, and there were people out there who had no idea that their lives had just been destroyed and that soon they'd get a phone call.

The following day, Jen was disturbed about the death, so she decided to move again. This time to Miami. Where she felt she could make a fresh start.

Her first day in Miami, sitting at the pool, Jen made a heroin friend. They went to his apartment and shot up heroin. Jen spent all her free time at his apartment. She couldn't stop using heroin and drinking until she blacked out.

One night she decided to commit suicide by jumping off the twentieth floor balcony. Fortunately, a friend stopped her and told her she needed to go back home and figure things out. She came home the next day. She was a mess. Her arms were infected and looked horrifying.

This was my first experience with one of my daughters using heroin. I can still remember that exact moment and how I sat on a chair in the living room. It felt like the ground was moving. I was in complete shock. Heroin? Really? This is something I've seen in movies. I've never actually known a person who used heroin. Heroin will kill you. And the people I saw in the movies on heroin were middle-aged men. They were homeless and greasy and very, very thin, with beards. Not pretty young girls.

We couldn't afford rehab, so Jen detoxed at home with us and began going to Alcoholics Anonymous meetings. All day. Every day. She was sober for more than four years.

Since her relapse, I've noticed several unexplained cuts on her arms and one on her face, and she has been forced, by law enforcement, into two different forty-eight hour psychiatric units. One in Phoenix and one in Los Angeles.

While she was sober, Jen got married, but when her husband went off the rails and spun out on crack and went to prison, she realized she was gay. Nothing will make you gay faster than hubby robbing a grocery store wearing a ski mask, cranked up on crack.

I walk into Jen's room. She's lying on her bed watching a movie, with a girl. Jen says, "Hi, Mom. I'm gay and this is my girlfriend."

I go, "Oh. Uhm. Nice to meet you." Then I walk out and say to John, "Hey, Jen is gay and that girl in there is her girlfriend."

He goes, "She's what?"

"Gay."

"She's gay?"

"Yeah. That's her girlfriend."

"Hum."

"Can you go get some milk? It's on sale at Fry's."

"Send Jen. And her girlfriend. They can be gay at Fry's."

Jen is gay. She has a girlfriend. Fine. They hold hands and hug each other. Fine. I couldn't care less. Let me say that the "girlfriends" are not making out in public or doing anything inappropriate. When we go to a mall, they walk around like any other couple.

Once, we went to a restaurant and they held hands. The entire restaurant turned to look at them like the girls had fire coming out of their asses. I ignored the other people and ate my meal.

Other times, I've heard comments. One old shriveled up lady said, "Why do the gays have to be affectionate in public?" I wanted to beat her down, but her wheelchair was in my way.

We go places and people pull their children away or cover their eyes. One man actually confronted them in a fast food restaurant.

Half the time, I ignore it. We have a good time anyway and just carry on with the day. But the other half of the time, I simply don't want to deal with it. I don't want to be stared at. I don't want to hear hurtful things. I don't want to feel like I have to defend them when we go somewhere. I feel like I'm being dishonest when I intentionally don't take the girls with me somewhere. But some days, I just don't want the look-at-the-gay-people attention.

Jen is an amazing, beautiful person. I want her to be happy and fall in love and laugh and cry and live a life. The gays are just like everyone else. But I'll be honest: when Jen and her girlfriend come over for dinner, I throw the silverware out after they leave. I don't want everyone in the house turning up gay.

April is twenty-eight. She is an alcoholic. I am an alcoholic, and the father of Jen and April is an alcoholic and an addict. If you bottle that up and produce children, odds are, the kids will have some issues.

But April's "issues" didn't show up until her late teens—as opposed to the other two girls who literally went from the play-pen to the crack den. April was the responsible one. She was organized, efficient, and on honor roll. April was that kid in school who reminded the teacher to give homework.

April was nineteen and living in Albuquerque. I had been told that she was hanging around with some really rough people. One day she called me and told me she was pregnant.

Finally. I didn't think I was ever going to get to be a grand-mamma.

We had a huge fight. I told her she should not have a child at nineteen. I told her I was speaking from experience and, as the saying goes, as hard as you think it's going to be, you end up wishing it were that easy. We fought and fought for several weeks. In the end it was clear: she was going to have a baby.

So I had to consciously change my way of thinking. I had to support her decision. It was hard. I didn't want my daughter to have a hard life. I knew what it was like trying to take care of a baby alone. She said the baby's father was great. They loved each other. He would be there and support her and take care of her—you know, all the things you hear before the baby arrives.

So the months went by. John and I slowly began to get excited about the prospect of becoming grandparents. Every time we went into a store, we picked up a few things. Lotion, oils, diapers, baby stuff. Then April found out her baby would be a boy, and she decided his name would be Moses, just like his father.

John immediately began to equip Moses with every kind of Chicago Cubs gear he could find. Moses would be a Cubs fan. As days and weeks went by, the excitement grew.

I talked to April daily. She took her pregnancy very seriously. No sweets, no soda, no bad food, only healthy things. She told me she had a headache, and I told her to take a Tylenol or Advil. She said absolutely not. No pills. She was pregnant and those pills would get into the baby's system. She did all the things her midwife and the hospital suggested. She took the classes, took the tour of the hospital. I was really proud of April. She read so many books on parenting and baby books, and really tried to get as much information as she could to be the best possible mom. She completely walked the line when she was pregnant.

The big day was approaching. We were so excited we couldn't stand it. Jen went to New Mexico to be with April in the delivery room. I was in Phoenix. They were going to call me as soon as I became a grandmother. Everything was set. All we needed was a baby named Moses.

Jen and April are in the delivery room. The baby is delivered, but then the doctors and nurses say "code blue." Moses has his umbilical cord wrapped around his neck three times.

Jen is standing there in shock and April doesn't know what's going on. Several people rush into the room and take Moses away. Jen runs out into the hallway and throws up on the floor. April is screaming, "What's going on? Someone tell me what's happening!"

I get a call from my ex-husband's sister, who is also at the hospital. She sounds strange. I can hear a lot of activity in the background. She says she doesn't know what is happening. She says they took Moses to another room. I'm confused and asking her questions. She says she will call back when she finds out what is going on.

April calls. She's crying and says there's something wrong with Moses. She says they took him to the intensive care unit. While she's on the phone, the doctor begins to tell her that the umbilical cord was wrapped around Moses' neck. April asks, "What does that mean? Is he going to be okay?" She says to me, "I have to go, Mom." And hangs up.

A while later, Jen calls and sounds completely shaken. She says the doctor doesn't know if Moses will survive. Moses is having a seizure. One long, never-ending seizure. They put him on three different seizure medications and a breathing machine because he can't breathe on his own.

John and I drive to Albuquerque at four in the morning. We walk into the baby intensive care unit, and I see April sitting by her son.

She looks up and sees us and starts to cry. She looks old. She looks completely broken down. She is pale and has dark circles under her swollen eyes.

*John and I walk around the corner, afraid of what we
will see, and there is tiny Moses. He is attached to so many
machines you can hardly see him. We can't kiss him. We can't
move him. All we can do is sit by him and rub his feet.*

They gave April a room in the intensive care unit so she could be close to her baby. The doctor met with us in her room and said he didn't know what was going to happen. He said the fact that Moses lived through the night was encouraging. We asked about long-term problems. The doctor said he didn't know. He said Moses was not out of the woods yet, and we would know more day-by-day.

Each day Moses got a little better. John and I had been there a week, and at that point the doctors felt confident Moses would survive. No one could say what problems he would have, and Moses had still not woken up once since he was born. Even so, John and I had to get back to our jobs before we got fired.

The day before we left, we stayed late at the hospital with April. When it was time for us to leave, April walked us out and here is another memory that will stick in my head forever: John and I were driving away, and in the rearview mirror I could see April standing on the sidewalk as the snow fell. Just standing there with her arms crossed with the snow falling on her face. My daughter, a mom, with a very sick baby.

Moses is eight now. He is in charge of every person in the house. He can't talk, but he has managed to become very bossy. With his left hand he summons you to come to him. He kisses you and then he actually points for you to go away. What he's saying is, "I'm done with you. Walk away."

He is so, so handsome and lovable. Moses has cerebral palsy. They said he wouldn't live. He's alive. They said he would never breathe on his own. He plays basketball with his grandfather. They said he wouldn't walk. He actually doesn't walk. He runs. Everywhere. I always say to him, "Moses, slow down. You don't have to run. You can walk." He looks at me and runs off.

He gives me so many kisses that I say it's a fine line between giving Grandma kisses and Grandma being charged with a felony.

We are madly in love with Moses, and Moses is madly in love with himself. He teaches us more in a day than we can teach him in a lifetime. He is always happy, always smiling, and his spirit can bring you up no matter what you're going through. Moses is the center of our world.

Moses wears a leg brace on his right leg. One day in a sporting goods store we were standing in line. There were two little boys about Moses' age standing in front of us with their father.

One boy said to the other, "He's got a plastic leg."

I leaned down and whispered, "It gives him super powers."

The boys began to pull on their father's pants. "Dad. I want that." Pointing at Moses' leg brace. The dad ignored them. They started crying, "Dad! I want it! I want super powers!"

Moses stood there staring at them. Super powers are something you're born with, not something you buy off a store shelf.

After Moses' traumatic birth, April's alcohol issues surfaced, and she has used alcohol to cope with life ever since. It is what it is. April has hardened. She will verbally rip us into pieces. If she has to, she will attack us physically. She's gone after John on several occasions and, I hate to say, almost won a few times.

The pain is eating her alive. We walk around on eggshells to stay clear of Hurricane April. She tells me she hates me, and that I never should have been a mother. I tell her that I thought I'd be better at it. It's like a job you think you'll excel at then you begin work and you completely suck. I know she doesn't mean it, but it's hurtful, and God knows I've given her plenty of ammunition.

On the outside, you'd never know April's pain. Perfect hair, makeup, perfectly put together outfits, gorgeous, driving a great car. All the latest purses and sunglasses.

And Moses is always in top fashion. He is the best-dressed child I have ever seen in my life. They both walk through life looking like a magazine cover. They live in a great house that is beautifully furnished, and April keeps it perfectly clean, always. You'd never know how sad April is on the inside. She does what she has to do to survive. One day in the neurologist's office, the doctor said that Moses only uses half his brain.

April said, "So when he grows up he'll be right on track with other men."

I'm proud of April for any way she gets through the day. She's a strong, strong young woman.

Carly, my youngest daughter. She was born old.

She made her own money by the time she was ten. She sold lemonade. She sat out there for hours and came in with sixty dollars and sometimes more. She watered down the lemonade so her lemonade and sugar would last longer.

I said, "But you are selling watery lemonade, and these people are paying for it!"

She said, "What are they gonna say, Mom? I'm a kid."

She changed religions. One day she was a Buddhist, and the next she was an atheist.

I said, "Don't you believe in God?"

She was nine and she said, "There's just no proof, Mom."

We went into art stores, and she told me about Vincent Van Gogh. Sometimes I have wondered if I took home the wrong baby. I wonder if there is a young girl in a five million dollar house somewhere craving Spam and wondering why.

At one point she became a vegetarian. She was on honor roll. Her teachers loved her, and she was in the popular crowd. She was gorgeous. She was funny.

I told Carly to be home by ten o'clock. She said, "By law, the curfew is eleven."

She asked if we would buy her a stereo if she cleaned her room every day until a certain date. We said okay. She went to her room and came back out with a completely written out contract for us to sign: "If Carly cleans her room every day until the fifth of March, we will buy her a stereo," and then "sign here."

Sometimes we had three or four contracts active at the same time. She taped them to her wall. If we tried to back out of a deal, she marched us into her room, pointed at the wall, and said, "What does this say?"

She started smoking pot at the age of twelve. Soon after—this is in middle school—kids brought various pills they had stolen from their parents' medicine cabinets. Painkillers, Xanax, anything that would make them high. We didn't have any pills at our house (yet), so Carly brought money, stolen out of my purse or her father's wallet.

By her first year of high school, Carly was taking so many of these pills that she got sick when she didn't have them.

One day, Carly came into my room and told me she needed to talk to me. She was fourteen. She said, "I need help." She was crying. "I have been using OxyContin every day for a year and I can't stop."

At that moment I had no fear because I had no idea what OxyContin was. I was confused. She said OxyContin was a very strong painkiller. I still had no fear. I thought, Just stop taking it. She told me she had to have it as soon as she woke up or she got really sick.

Then I thought back over the previous year. There were so many times I heard Carly throwing up in the morning. She got really bad headaches, and she was losing weight. A lot of weight.

I called the number on my insurance card and made an appointment at a detox facility. The detox facility said that Oxy-Contin was extremely popular and use of this particular drug had skyrocketed over the past five years. They said it was a good thing I brought her in and no, she could not detox off this drug at home. I suddenly realized the gravity of Carly's situation. She was in a shitload of trouble.

Then we met with a doctor after Carly had spoken with him privately. He used the word "heroin."

I said, "Wait. Did you say heroin?"

Carly said, "I only used it a few times."

I said, "Heroin?" I felt like I was in another world again. Something in my head said, This can't be happening. But this is the end of it. Carly will detox, and then we'll get on with our lives. After all, this is what happened with Jen—only Jen was twenty-three, not fourteen. Jen stopped. Carly would stop, too.

Carly's boyfriend was also using, but he promised he would

also stop. So there you have it. They would both stop because it was ridiculous to just continue doing this. This will kill you. So they would both stop. I was so proud of them.

Carly's boyfriend was a really sweet guy. He wasn't what you picture a drug addict to be. He was handsome, and so, so intelligent. They were together every second of the day. He was polite and courteous, and he went on family vacations with us. He was also using this OxyContin. We talked to him about it, but he assured us he was never going to take drugs again. We believed him. I think he actually believed himself.

Carly went through detox four times before the insurance company would finance an inpatient rehab. She went to the thirty-day rehab, and her boyfriend wrote letters talking about how he was clean and how much he missed her. How they were going to stay clean together. It all sounded very sweet, and looking back, I just wanted to believe that was the case. They would stay clean. The day she got out of rehab, Carly said she wanted to see him immediately.

This was typical of my decision-making skills. I look back and know I was a special kind of stupid.

I instinctively knew it was not a good idea to let them see each other, but I didn't follow my instincts. I dropped her off for an hour while I ran some errands.

Even as I read that, I am kicking myself in the ass. I dropped her off with the kid she used drugs with. They promised not to use drugs anymore. They fucking promised! And I looked at their faces and believed them! The day a heroin addict can look you straight in the eye and flat out lie is a sad day for the world.

I got a call a half hour later saying they were going to a movie. During the course of Carly's drug use, the "I'm going to a movie" line would be used hundreds of times. And, of course, I only have my stupidity to blame. Two days later I noticed Carly was sleeping twelve hours a day, but now I knew to check to be sure she was breathing.

I know there are other parents of alcoholics and addicts who will understand when I say the words, "Carly has to decide to be clean or not. It's up to her." But I feel sick when I say that. I know she has to be the one to make the choice to stay clean. But I don't think I'm the only parent in the world who is thinking, I will take care of this. Because this is what we do as parents.

It starts when they are little babies. The tears come and you pick her up and bounce her or spin her until she laughs. Whatever comes up, we try to fix it. We just want her smiling all the time.

She gets older and the boy doesn't like her back…he likes her friend. So we buy her clothes and take her to a movie. And just like that, she is "fixed."

Now we are on a journey, but we cannot take this journey together. I know for Carly to successfully recover I have to dump the entire bag of shit on her lap. She has to venture out on her own and make it happen, or, God forbid, not make it happen. And I hate that. The idea makes me ill.

One day, I said to Carly, "You know, I've done all I can. It's up to you now."

She smiled that pretty smile and said, "Sorry, Mom. But it's always been up to me."

I thought I could make her better. With love. Am I the only one? Do other parents try this exhausting road making them stay clean with "love"?

Another thing I'm guilty of is thinking, If she has a Coach purse like the other girls, she will stop using heroin. I can't count the number of times I've heard drug addicts say, "I was a heroin addict, then I got a Coach purse and never used heroin again."

I'm sure when Carly and I were walking through a mall people thought she was an average teenage girl. And I liked that feeling of being just like everyone else. A mom and her daughter out for the day searching for the perfect trendy item so the daughter wouldn't use heroin that day.

We went on like this for years. She eventually broke up with the boyfriend. We were relieved but also silently worried that he would overdose. He may be a drug addict, but he is a good person deep inside, and we were always fearful about getting that call. Carly worried too. I think she still does.

OxyContin is expensive, so my daughter and her group of friends found out that heroin had the same effect as OxyContin and was much cheaper. So they supplemented their OxyContin use with heroin until their use elevated to the level that they could only afford heroin. They had to stay high all day or they would become very, very sick. They would smoke it off tinfoil. Carly and a couple of the other kids also found out that if they injected it, the high is much more intense.

Many of the kids, including my daughter, injected heroin with crystal meth. So they were in even deeper—so deep that it's almost impossible to ever get back.

There were ten or twelve kids in this group, and all of their lives have been destroyed. Two young people my daughter knew died of overdoses.

Carly has been in intensive care three times because of overdoses. She has been to rehab, doctors, outpatient, inpatient, and detox nine times.

One night after a week-long drug binge, my beautiful seventeen-year-old daughter said, "Mom. I'm already dead. I'm just stuck here."

Every single inpatient treatment Carly has received was only because I didn't accept their refusal to treat her.

Every insurance company in the world will first approve what they call "a lower level of care." The translation is, "We are saving money by not medically treating your child." Fight, scream, cry, do whatever you have to do to get help for your children. They deserve help. They desperately need help.

Carly is nineteen now and has not been to school since she was thirteen. She has never worked or had a driver's license or had anything or done anything that other people do. She didn't smoke pot in junior high school and progress to other drugs as she got older. She smoked pot one day and it seems like she was smoking heroin the next. There is a slang term for smoking heroin: Chasing the dragon. That's when Carly began circling the drain. And because she was so young, it all unfolded in front of our eyes as we watched in horror.

In the last couple of years, our daughter's drug use has sent us crumbling to the floor in fear and desperation more times than I can remember.

I've made so many mistakes. Obvious mistakes. Did I really think Carly was clean? Or was the truth just too painful for my brain to comprehend? I don't know. Both, I guess.

At our house, our lives are in two parts: before Carly started using, and after. The other day, walking through a parking lot,

I thought, I just want my daughter back. The way she used to be. And then I realized, I don't remember how she used to be. I don't remember most conversations, most events. I don't remember holidays or birthdays. I don't remember the little things that people remember about their kids when they were growing up. It has been so traumatic watching her drug addiction progress that my memory from before is gone.

I do remember her weeks in intensive care...her seizures and vomiting...her stays in detox and rehab. And I remember watching her when she was psychotic from meth and cowering in the corner of the dark laundry room because the helicopters were coming to get her. A ninety-pound stranger. Watching and feeling that I had lost her. The "her" she was—my beautiful, beautiful girl—now someone else, something else.

God,

Thank you for all the gifts in my life. My husband, my beau-tiful daughters, my perfect grandson, and my mother. Thank you for guiding me day-by-day in this difficult part of my life. Thank you for courage to face my challenges, and grace during my victories.

Please God, wrap your arms around my family so they know we will be safe because you are walking with us. I know you are watching over us because we're all still here. That, in itself, is a miracle, and I thank you and try to have gratitude in my heart everyday. Because of you I am able to cry, but also able to laugh.

I have three issues on my prayer agenda today. One. They say you don't give us more than we can handle. I feel that you've mistaken me for someone else. You've mistaken me for a really strong person like Angelina Jolie, the Mia Farrow of our generation.

The truth is I'm not able to handle all of this ridiculous crap. I am not Madonna or Oprah or Kelly Ripa. I'm just a person.

Two. My foul mouth. Every time I say a curse word, I feel like you're looking down at me like a parent would, still loving me, but thinking, Why does she have to use that language?

That's just the way I talk. I don't think I can stop. The foul language doesn't feel like anything to me. The word I really like is the F-word. I'm very heavy on that word. I also like saying *"shit sack." I use these words as verbs, nouns, and adjectives for just about everything I'm describing. It's just the way I talk. And I know you love me anyway. But as far as being a better person, to stop with the foul language is not something that I can do. Someday I will. Just not today. And not tomorrow.*

The third thing and most important: if there is any way I could get that government stimulus check sooner, I would have complete gratitude. I know a lot of people are asking you for this, but you know my situation. I really need the cash.

I have previously prayed to win the lottery and of course, that prayer still stands.

Thank you for all the miracles in my life. Without you, I would be lost. And you've seen me lost. It's ugly.

Amen.

Assault, Mary Jane, and
a Prior Conviction

*I wish someone had told me what would come later. I mean, on
down the road. I could have been better prepared. I wish someone had told me that kids become drug addicts. And they almost
die. And when that happens, a piece of you is gone and you feel
it leaving. You dig your feet in and focus, but the whole time the
ground is moving. The blue lips, the beeping of the equipment
monitoring your kid's breath. And all you can do is watch.*

*I wish someone had told me what would come later.
Watching that kid try to pick up the pieces of her life from off
the ground. Piece by piece. Her eyes red and tired—her spirit
asleep. And you want to help, but you can't. She has to pick up
the pieces by herself. Some of the pieces are as sharp as broken
glass, but she has to pick them up anyway so nothing will be
missing when she's done. Piece by painful piece—only to drop
them on the ground again.*

*I wish someone had told me that this would become the
way we live…watching the pieces fall to the floor, watching
the kid pick them up again…and actually praying to God every
minute that this kid will be able to pick them up one more time.*

And I wish I knew the magic thing to say or do to make it stop.
Should I love her more or love her less…should I do this or not
do that…and on and on as I fall asleep at night. Every night.

I wish someone had told me what would come later. That
we would have to learn to live in it. We still work, pay our bills,
eat dinner. We watch movies, go on trips, take a swim. We
laugh, cry, fight. Some days are good, some not so good. Sort of
like before, but not really. I hope someday the fear will fall away.
Hope is the main thing. Love them, kiss them, and have hope. I
wish someone had told me.

Carly was sixteen and an intravenous heroin addict on state-funded medical insurance. So the state sent a caseworker to my house to see Carly and report back on her condition so they could take the appropriate steps.

The caseworkers are professionals for troubled teenagers who are "experimenting" with drugs. The state is not equipped to assist serious drug addicts who are under eighteen. The state emphasizes counseling, which doesn't work so well with an adolescent heroin/meth addict.

It was clear that this particular caseworker hadn't run into the likes of a sixteen-year-old chronic drug addict like Carly. He was a tall, very slim, balding, twenty-two-year-old guy with dress slacks pulled up above his belly button. He was on a one-man mission to save kids from drugs and bad behavior, but most of the kids he saw were involved in bad behavior, not drugs. Now here he was, face-to-face with Carly, who was withdrawing from heroin. He was actually holding in his hand the physiology books he had just been reading.

As with many people in this book, I can't say his real name or feelings will be hurt. So let's call him Lenny. Lenny was in way over his head.

Lenny pulls me aside and whispers, "I'm going to try a technique called 'mirroring.' It's where Carly says something and I repeat it so she feels that I understand her."

I whisper, "Okay." Lenny and Carly sit at the kitchen table. I stand at a distance on the other side of the kitchen.

Lenny says to Carly, "It's a real treat to see you, Carly! You look fantastic!"

Carly stares at him with a green face, eight-five pounds and dark circles under her eyes, but makes an effort at her manners. "Yeah. Thanks. It's nice for you to come and see me."

Lenny: "So…it's nice for me to come and see you?"

Carly: "Uhm, yeah."

Lenny: "So, yes?"

Carly: "I'm sorry. What are you asking me?"

Lenny: "So you're sorry and what am I asking you?"

Lenny looks over at me and winks as if he's really plowing through Carly's mental minefield with the mirroring. Carly could have a seizure at any point during the mirroring process. Her arms are infected, and I am not completely sure she is even aware that Lenny is in the house much less mirroring her every word.

Lenny begins to talk really loudly and slowly, as if Carly is deaf: "Carly! We have some activities that we would like you to be involved in! Does that make sense?"

I cut in: "You know, Lenny, we were hoping you were making arrangements to get Carly into an inpatient program…"

Lenny waves me off. "It's in the works, it is. I'm just think-ing until that happens we could get Carly doing some really fun activities." Again speaking really loudly and slowly: "Carly? Would you like to do some fun activities?"

Carly, staring out the window: "Activities?"

Lenny: "Activities?" There is a long pause because he's still mirroring but he has nothing to mirror. "Yes. Activities."

I can't stand it and I interrupt again. "Okay, Lenny, listen. I don't know what activities you're talking about, but Carly is really sick and needs to be in a drug rehab…"

Lenny holds his hand up again. "I know this. But until then I have some ideas. Carly. Numero uno. Camping with some great kids who are your age—and of course that includes a lot of ter-rific water activities. Two. Picnic in the park. And three, saving the best for last, Cosmic Bowling! Carly? What do you say we get our Cosmic Bowling on?"

Carly, still staring out the window: "I'm tired."

I really can't take anymore. "Listen to me, Lenny. She needs help. She needs treatment. How long is it going to take to make it happen?"

Lenny crosses his legs and says, "How long is it going to…"

"Don't mirror me. How long?"

"Well, four to six weeks. That's our process. We always hope the youth will decide not to take drugs anymore by doing some of the fun activities."

"Listen, Lenny. Carly could be dead in four weeks."

Lenny walks over to me and whispers, "We don't like to use the 'dead' word. It may be the most negative word ever."

I whisper, "Yes. It's very negative. But so is using heroin ten times a day."

Carly: "I think I better go lie down."
Lenny, as Carly is walking out of the room: "So you think
you better go lie down?"

Carly has asked me a thousand times, "Why did God make me this way?"

I don't know how to answer that. I've asked myself the same question. But I don't really think God made her this way. I think it's a hundred different things. One of the pieces is me. The drinking, screaming, and the long list of things I could have done better. Another piece is Carly's dad. Another piece is Carly's sisters. And on and on.

The best way to know if you're making the right decision as a parent is to ask people who don't have children. For some reason these people have the answer for every situation. They would do this, or they would do that. This wouldn't have happened if you had done it this way. They're the same people who say, "I don't have any children, but I completely understand because I have a cat."

Let me explain this loud and clear: having a cat or a dog or a yak is nothing like having a child. You will never have to pay for drug rehab for your yak. I could not put my child in a crate while I went to work. Actually, I could have, and looking back, I probably should have. But it's illegal.

Your dog will never scream at you, "I hate you!" and go into his dog house and slam the door.

Your cat will never date a felon. And it's not because she has higher standards. It's because she's a cat.

Amazingly enough, the same people are experts on drug and alcohol addiction. They have all the answers. Don't take drugs.

Or, if your kid is on drugs, kick his ass. Or get her into a sport. Throw her out on the street without her clothes and tell her you won't be her parent anymore.

John and I tried all these things and none of them worked. We should have used the crate.

————— ⟨⟨⟩⟩ —————

I'd like to pretend this next incident didn't happen. Carly was at a party doing heroin with her new drug dealer boyfriend, "Phil." The police showed up at the house. Carly had several packages of heroin wrapped in tinfoil in her pocket. She swallowed them so the police wouldn't find them.

The next morning we were sitting with her in the intensive care unit. She was unconscious except for an occasional mumble that wasn't actual words. The doctors said they couldn't get an exact answer as to how much heroin she swallowed, so they didn't know what would happen when the heroin dissolved through the tin-foil. They said she could overdose right in her hospital bed.

They told us if we had family that lived other places, we might want to call them so they could come and be with us if something happened. There was again a nurse posted by Carly's bed twenty-four hours a day.

The nurse walked in the room. At this point John and I had been clean of alcohol and drugs for almost six years. The nurse did her nurse thing, and then put her hands on her gigantic hips and said to me and John, "Where in the world were you two while all this was going on?"

John and I stared at her with dark circles under our eyes, filled with complete desperation and sadness. Our hearts completely and utterly broken. We were so broken we couldn't even defend ourselves. And at the exact same time, I had been thinking, Where was I when all this was going on?

Carly stayed in that unit for seven or eight days until they said she had passed the foil or it had dissolved. So they discharged her. The hospital gave us medication for heroin withdrawal to help Carly "sleep it off." They said we absolutely had to keep her under complete lock and key because between the heroin and the withdrawal medication, if she used street drugs on top of that she would overdose. They said it over and over: Do not let her out of your sight. She will overdose if she uses with all that her system has been through.

They said we should check her into a drug rehab straight from the hospital. But when we said we couldn't pay for a drug rehab, the hospital came up empty handed as far as any rehab that would take Carly without a giant pile of cash. I asked if it was a bad idea to release Carly in this condition, but they waved their hands and said she was okay.

So they rolled her out in a wheelchair, and we put her in the car because she was hardly able to stand up. She fell asleep in the backseat on the way home. When we got home, we called rehabs and got the same answer at each one: no money, no medical treatment.

That night we gave Carly the medication to help her sleep even though she wasn't really awake. We just wanted to be sure she would pass out for the night, and the doctor said that was what we should do. She took it and she was out. She was really, really out.

John and I went to bed and thanked God for saving her. Again.

Three o'clock in the morning: Jen walked into our room and said, "She's gone."

At first I thought Jen meant Carly was dead. We jumped up and ran to her room. Carly was gone. She was fucking GONE! Now we were all up, pacing and screaming. How did she leave? Who did she go with? She couldn't even stand up! All her clothes were gone! The bottle of pills that the hospital gave us was gone.

The next morning, I had to go to work because I had already taken the week before off to sleep at the hospital with Carly. At my job, I was under constant threat of being fired. I did not like my boss, and my boss did not like me. That was fine with both of us. As with other people in this book, I don't want to hurt feelings so I've changed his name. In this book I will call my boss "Ballsack."

When I went to work, Jen and April went online and got Carly's cell phone records. The night before, there were several incoming calls from the drug dealer boyfriend, Phil. And some outgoing calls to Phil. So Carly was with Phil. He had come and picked her up in the middle of the night after we had all fallen asleep. She had packed a bag with everything she owned, took a thousand dollars out of her father's wallet—rent money that John was going to deposit—and now Carly and Phil were gone with the rent money.

Let me say something about Carly's cell phone. Many people would say that if their kid was using drugs, the cell phone would be the first thing to go. But as time passed, there were times when the only way to get to her was through that cell phone. That doesn't mean she would answer it. But she would get our messages, and if we said just the right thing at just the right time, she would call us back and we could go pick her up. Most of the time that was our only line to our daughter. Without the cell phone, we felt completely cut off from her. And remember, she was sixteen, not twenty-five. If nothing else it made me feel better to at least call and leave a message saying, I love you, that's all. I love you.

I'm standing at my register, and I'm getting text messages from home—even though I've signed a paper saying I wouldn't use my cell phone at my register. But I have to take the chance so I can get information about Carly.

I get a text from Jen saying, "We found out where Phil's parents live. Me and April and Dad are driving over there."

I feel panic and drop the phone in my pocket. Another employee comes up to me and says, "Ballsack wants you in his office."

I walk in and there is Ballsack and another manager. Ballsack tells the other manager to shut the door, and then says to me, "Have a seat."

I sit.

Ballsack, crossing his arms and pacing back and forth: "Can you tell me what your PSS is?"

Me: "Uhm. What is a PSS?"

Ballsack: "You've worked here nine years and you don't know what a PSS is?"

Me: "I'm sorry. Maybe if you said the words instead of the letters..."

Ballsack: "PSS. Personal Service Score."

My phone vibrates with another text message. My stomach rolls with panic. "Wow. I'm sorry. What was the question?"

Ballsack: "What is your Personal Service Score?"

"Oh. Thirty-seven?"

Ballsack: "No. Eighty."

"Oh, wow! Eighty! Eighty is good. Right?"

Ballsack: "Is that how you live your life? Eighty percent? That's good enough for you? Is that what you give your family? Eighty percent?"

"I actually only give my family thirty percent."

Complete silence. My phone vibrates again.

Ballsack: "I'm going to have to ask for that other twenty percent."

"Okay."

Ballsack: "Okay, so, when you make eye contact with a customer, what percentage of those times do you smile and say 'Good Morning' or 'Hello, how are you today?'"

"Eighty percent. Just kidding. One hundred percent."

Complete silence.

Ballsack, handing me a piece of paper: "Sign this acknowledging that we had this conversation. And if you have to sign two more papers because you're twenty percent short of what is required of you, you will be fired."

"I am hearing you. One hundred percent." I sign the paper. Every time I turn around at work I am signing another piece of paper.

While I'm signing, my phone vibrates again. I walk back to my register and check my messages.

Phil was the first person to teach Carly to shoot up drugs. The first several times, he had to do it for her, but then she learned. He also was more into meth than heroin. After Phil picked up Carly in the middle of the night, he told her she should shoot up heroin and meth if she wanted to get completely high. After all they had a thousand dollars. But they ran through that money quickly paying drug dealers who wanted to kill Phil, so they had to make more money. So they were selling drugs and guns. Phil told Carly that she needed to carry all the drugs and whatever gun they were selling because if they got pulled over, the police wouldn't search Carly. Fuck bag.

We called Carly and Phil, and left messages pleading with Carly to come home. We told Phil that Carly was sick…that she could die if she took any more drugs…and that if he cared about her at all, he would just drop her off somewhere, and we would go and pick her up.

Once Phil answered the phone and told John to "fuck off." After a short time both their phone mailboxes were full.

We called the police because we wanted to have Carly arrested. The police officer told us he couldn't arrest her. He said she's not doing anything. We explained her week in intensive care and what the doctors told us. We begged, but he said he wouldn't look for her.

John began screaming and told the police officer, "I hope you never have to experience this kind of pain!"

The police officer said he wouldn't because he was teaching his kids to have morals.

We hoped Phil's parents would talk to Phil and persuade him to bring Carly home. We called. They hung up. So John and Jen and April found their address and went to their house. Phil's mom screamed that she was going to call the police. John said we were just trying to find our daughter. Phil's mom called the police, so John, Jen, and April left. Quickly.

It's difficult to explain the terror we were feeling right then. All I could hear in my head was the doctor saying Carly would die. We were all terrified—completely desperate to get her home. So we went on Carly's MySpace page where there was a picture of Carly and, by luck, a picture of Phil. We made flyers with both their pictures that said, "If you see either of these people please call…" and left our phone numbers. We put them up all over the city. We also put them up by Phil's parents' house hoping this would pressure them into calling Phil.

We put the flyers in convenience stores in the heavily drug-populated areas, in grocery store windows, everywhere.

We start getting calls, but not the kind of calls we were expecting. We got calls from several drug dealers saying if they found Carly they'd bring her home, but Phil owed them money and he was as good as dead. We also got several calls from people who said Phil invaded their homes and held them at gun point and stole all their drugs.

I'm on my register getting updates and Ballsack walks by: "So where's today's smile? Remember your smile is part of your uniform!"

I smile. Because it's part of my uniform.

My cell number was also on the flyer. I am standing at my register and my phone vibrates. As I scan groceries, I glance down and see that the number doesn't look familiar.

I smile at my customer, and then I stop scanning, kneel down behind my register, and answer my phone.

A man says, "If I find your daughter, I'll get her to you. But I will put a bullet in Phil's head first."

I say, "Okay then. Thanks."

I hang up the phone and stand up. My stomach is churning. I smile again at my customer who is now glaring at me with hate. I

scan and say, "So did you find everything you needed today?"
Ballsack walks by and I smile because it's part of the uniform.

We got one call from a single mother who had to move all the way across town because Phil had done the same thing with her daughter. When she finally got her daughter back, Phil drove by their home and shot out all their front windows. There were several calls from people who said Phil had shot up their houses.

The phone rang off the hook with Phil stories. These stories only made us more fearful for Carly. Now we were out of our minds with worry. Then we got the phone call that started the most insane movement from our house that I have ever experienced.

It was in the middle of the night. It was a girl who used to date Phil. She saw one of the flyers and said she still saw Phil on occasion. She said she could convince him to meet her, and that would give us an opportunity to grab Carly.

The girl called Phil and told him to meet her at a convenience store in the middle of the "hood." I would go so far as to say it was in the "hood of the hood." The only reason you would go to this area would be to buy heroin or meth. The girl called back and told us Phil agreed to meet her there.

John, Jen, and April were walking out the door, and I was screaming, "Are you people crazy? You're going to get shot!"

April said, "Not until I kick his fucking ass into the ground." Now April was on the case and I was actually worried about Phil. They walked out. Holy God.

I have been married to John for twenty years. He has never been in a physical altercation with anyone. Ever. Never even close.

But something about your children does things to your brain. And John's patience for Phil was gone.

They got to the convenience store and met the girl. They introduced themselves as if they were at a cocktail party. The girl said she would bring Phil around the back of the store, so John and the girls went to hide behind the store in the dark. The last thing the girl said to John was, "Be careful. Phil always carries a gun." Great.

Phil pulls up in front of the store. He gets out of the car, and tucks something in the front of his jeans. John is sure it's a gun. John looks down and sees a big stick lying by the trash dumpster. John picks up the stick.

The gun is a problem, but the bigger problem is that Phil did not bring Carly with him. Phil and the girl walk around behind the store where the gang with the stick is hiding. When Phil is two steps away, John clocks him with the stick. Phil goes down and the girls start kicking him and screaming, "Tell me where my sister is, you shit bag!" John is now thinking the girls may kill Phil.

John tries to pull the crazy girls off of Phil. Jen backs off right away, but April wants a few more shots.

Someone in the apartments next to the parking lot calls the police. The police show up. Phil is wrecked.

John explains what has happened for the last week and about trying to find Carly. Phil sits on the curb saying he doesn't even know Carly, although he's wearing her belt. The police are going to arrest John and the girls for assault. John is now really pissed off because he's going to jail. He tells Phil, "We'll meet again. Think about it this way: I only brought the B team this time. Two girls. Next time you won't be that lucky."

Now the police say they are adding charges because John is threatening Phil. April is smarter and is not so direct with Phil. She says things like, "You should go to beauty school or do nails."

The police say we should have just called the police in the first place. John says we did. Three times. They told us there was nothing they could do, and said we should have raised Carly with morals. The police handcuff John, Jen and April, but then Phil says he doesn't want to press charges. He just wants to go home.

After a long scolding from the police, Stick Man and Girls Gone Wild are let go with a stern warning: "You are not police officers."

The next morning, a bruised-up Phil got back to whatever crack den Carly and he were living in. He told Carly, "You have to get out of here. Your family is crazy, and I can't be dealing with this. Get your shit and get out."

So seven days after Carly escaped in the middle of the night, the phone rang and it was her, crying, "Can someone come and pick me up? I'm walking down a street with my bag. It's heavy."

We picked up Carly and brought her home. She had been shooting up meth the entire time she was gone. We called every detox center we could think of, but there were no beds. Meth addiction is on the bottom of the list for beds because they say there is no physical danger from withdrawing from meth. So every place we called, no bed. We called about twenty rehabs and begged. We pleaded. We cried. But no money, no treatment. So we had to detox Carly off meth ourselves. At home.

This time we had to make absolutely sure Carly didn't leave

the house. So we had to watch her in shifts. Someone had to be awake all the time and be right with her. Every time Carly hallucinated, talked crazy, became enraged, and tried to get out the front door, she was met by a family member physically restraining her. But it was too much for us. We needed help. So we called Andy.

Carly had met Andy in Narcotics Anonymous. I knew the minute she met him she was completely infatuated. Andy is really good-looking, funny and charming. Carly ate it all up.

Andy got a job with my husband, and Andy became very close to our family. He was clean from opiates by taking a drug called Suboxone. The Suboxone worked, but there is always the other side of the coin. It's very difficult to get Suboxone and it's very expensive. It's also very hard to get off Suboxone, so it turns out to be another chemical problem. But it seemed to be working for Andy.

Carly was relapsing during the time she was with Andy, and they broke up when Carly relapsed. But every time she promised to stay clean, they got back together.

During the time that Carly was in the hospital and then on the run with Phil, Andy was out of the picture. But we knew Andy was clean because he was working for John. So we called Andy for help. Andy still loved Carly. He said he would come and keep her in the house when we needed to go to sleep. Carly was high but thrilled that Andy would be her guard.

One way to look at addicts and alcoholics is the way you look at one of those Magic Eye hologram pictures they sell in the mall. When you first look at the picture, it's just colors and dots. But if you stand still and look past the surface, there is an actual picture of something—a girl on a bike, or a cat playing with yarn. That's how I look at people. At first, some people are just this confusing fucked-up mess. But if I'm still and look past the mess, I see something beautiful. Something deeper and more real than what I saw at first glance. And then, when I can see it clearly, I think, Why didn't I see that in the first place? It's so clear. You just have to be still and look past the mess. Although sometimes, I look at people and all I see is a cat playing with yarn.

We had a good system for watching Carly. Andy liked to stay up late, so he would watch Carly until 3:30 or 4:00 in the morning. John wakes up naturally at about that time (I don't know why), so then Andy would go to sleep. It was a good system, but we had two major problems.

One was waiting for Phil to drive by the house and shoot out the front windows. The front part of the house was the living room and one bedroom. The answer was to board up the windows. But we leased the house, so we had to board up the windows from the inside so the landlord didn't drive by and realize he had crazy people living in his house. No one could walk into the living room or bedroom, so we had to conduct life in the back of the house.

The second problem was that Carly was really, really out of her mind. I knew it would help if we could just get her to go to sleep, but meth keeps you up for days and days. I had medication that would put her to sleep, but I was worried about the overdose problem. I didn't know what to do. She was pacing around the house and having hallucinations that people were trying to take her or chase her or kill her.

So here is another proud mother moment that should be in a greeting card. I asked Jen and April to buy some pot for Carly. Marijuana. If nothing else, I thought it would take the edge off for Carly, and you can't overdose on pot. I didn't feel great about the idea, but I couldn't watch Carly be crazy anymore.

The girls went and got some pot, which I know is illegal but so is assault and we had already crossed that road. Trust me, if we say bring our daughter home, you should bring her home. You don't want April rolling up on your crack den when her sister is in there. April will assault you into submission and then feng shui your living room on the way out. It's called Divine Order.

I went into Carly's room. She was sitting in a corner and Andy was sitting on her bed. I gave her the Mary Jane and said, "Smoke pot." She grabbed it and lit up. Twenty minutes later she said it didn't help. I said smoke more.

Here's the fact: it eventually worked. Each day it worked better and better until the day I said okay, no more pot. Not because I'm a strict parent, but because we ran out. But for those couple of days, it saved us. I would say, Please eat something, then smoke pot.

So Carly would eat, smoke, eat, smoke. Three days later, the pot was gone, and she just started eating and sleeping. She finally began to come out of it. She started making sense and the hallucinations stopped. She came to me and John and said, "Thank you for not letting me go."

While all of this was happening, life was going on. It was Halloween. Everybody at work was dressing up, but not me because I'm not fun. I did go look at costumes one day, but the costumes for women were all sexy-slash-something. Sexy nurse. Sexy librarian. Sexy nun.

My failure as a mother was always clear at Halloween. While the better mothers handmade their children's elaborate costumes, I waited until noon Halloween day to go to the costume store. By that time, the shelves appeared to have been ripped apart by packs of wild wolves, and all that was left was pieces of different costumes. I would say to April, "What do you mean, 'What is it?' It's an eggplant costume. Put the clown shoes on with it so it will look really cute. Do you want to wear the Elvira wig, too, or no?"

Some years were worse than that. We couldn't even afford pieces of a costume. So I would put face makeup on the girls and buy one of those little containers that you put on your face to look like a scar. "What do you mean, 'What are you?' You're an infected cut! It's fun, right? Go! Get some candy!" One year I got a stick and glued a big piece of paper on it that read, "On Strike!" She was a picketer. Cute, right?

I was checking groceries, and I got a text from Jen. April's new boyfriend had beat April to a pulp. I faked sick and left work. I was sure I'd be signing a piece of paper the next day.

I went to April's house and she clearly had a concussion, but she refused to go to the hospital. I could see lumps all over her head and bruising all over her legs and arms. She also refused to come to my house where she would be safe.

April's house isn't far away, so for the next few days, John and I drove back and forth, trying to take care of Carly at our house and April at her house.

John and I were at home one day, and April's shit sack boyfriend called to tell us that we would never see our daughter again. In the background, we heard April screaming. Then the boyfriend hung up.

A while later, April called and said everything is fine. He was just mad. He was sweet as sugar now and sorry, and he bought her some gifts. But then he kicked the shit out of her again because she wasn't "listening."

April's boyfriend was a very violent person. Restraining orders didn't stop him, they encouraged him. So after he beat April again, John and I went to April's house, packed all her things into a U-Haul, and moved her to a different place where the psycho wouldn't be able to find her. Andy helped us.

I'm back at work, and John texts me to say, "He found April. Tried to choke her. Carly is asleep."

A short while later, I'm sitting in Ballsack's office signing a paper. A Secret Shopper said I didn't smile at her. Ballsack reminds me that a smile is part of the uniform.

Ten minutes later I hear Ballsack over the intercom: "Huddle to the break room!"

A huddle is where the boss calls us all in and tries to pump us up about groceries. This chain of grocery stores uses a lot of numbers and percentages, and if you were a one hundred percent employee, you knew these numbers. I, on the other hand, couldn't give fucking fuck about the numbers. I hate huddles. They are stupid. I don't give a shit what you say during the huddle. I'm only going to want to kill myself more when it's over.

Ballsack, pacing back and forth in the huddle: "Who knows our store average?"

Silence.

Ballsack: "Dina?"

"Well...(I knew it had a point in it)...forty-two point...I don't know."

Ballsack: "Seventy-six point four."

Me: "That's right."

Ballsack: "Who can tell me what our goal for the quarter was?"

Silence.

Ballsack: "Dina?"

My phone vibrates. I think I may vomit. I try mirroring: "What was our goal?"

Ballsack: "What was our goal! You know! Our goal!"

"Forty...."

Ballsack: "No! No! No! Eighty-one point six!" Then he launches into a ten minute thing about how we need to pretend the customers are our own flesh and blood, and if we don't want to do this, there are piles of applications from people who will do it. My phone is vibrating the entire time.

We end the huddle in the same motivating way we always do. We all stand in a circle, put a hand in, and shout something inspirational. Like, "We're number one!" or "I'm a team player!"

After the huddle I look at a text message on my phone. It says, "April says she loves him and there's nothing we can do about it."

That day, April invited the boyfriend to the new place. Weeks later we moved her again after another drunken, drug-fueled assault. But she invited him to the new place again. She said we simply had to support the fact that they were in love and were going to be together forever—or at least until he murdered her. We said we would not support her in this violent relationship. Shortly after that, he beat her again. So we moved her again. And April invited him over again. Not surprisingly, he beat her again. And we moved her again.

All in all, we moved April four times in less than a year. It only ended because the boyfriend went to prison for a prior conviction. Thank God for prior convictions.

But by the time the boyfriend went to prison, April's relationship with us was very strained. One evening, extremely intoxicated, she became angry with us, busted out all the windows on the front of our house, and then drove her SUV into the back of our Jeep, smashing it into the closed garage door. We had her arrested.

It was a bad night, and it was all because of alcohol. April may be aggressive when she's not drinking, but she never in a million years would have broken out our windows and rammed our car if she was sober. She is so, so gorgeous, and so intelligent. But the alcohol is going to sink her.

It's no different than Carly using heroin. Many people feel that alcohol is different from drugs, but it's the same. The only difference is that the commercials for alcohol are better. Alcoholics end up cradling the toilet just like heroin addicts. One isn't more glamorous than the other. They both suck.

My heart feels sad because these days it's hard for me to find April even when I'm looking right at her. I miss that funny little girl who would lend me money from her piggy bank and say, "I'm going to lend this to you, BUT there will have to be a little extra come my way when I get it back. I'm not a bank." She was ten. I was borrowing money from a ten-year-old.

After the attack with the stick, Andy was at our house for more than a week. At that point, he was exhausted and ready to go home.

Carly wasn't a fun person to be around, and moving April wasn't in the original plan. But Andy helped like he always does. Then he went home. We will always be thankful for his help.

Those were dark days. One reason they were dark was because all our windows were boarded up. But they were also dark because Carly was in the back room smoking Mary Jane prescribed by her mother. I think to myself, Did I really do that? Yes. I did. It was a horrible situation to be in.

Now the whole thing seems sort of funny. If someone needed something in the living room, they would crawl in there, grab it, and crawl back. I can envision them wearing full camouflage, with a helmet with a plant on top, crawling flat on their stomachs into the living room: "Cover me! I'm going in!" Just to get the new People magazine that was lying on the table.

The day after the assault with the stick, Phil's father called. He said they were pressing charges against us for assaulting Phil. Judging by the four million dollar house they lived in, I immediately assumed they had the resources to do that. Phil's father and I screamed on the phone back and forth for about fifteen minutes.

Then I said something about Carly meaning everything to me. Phil's father became quiet. He said he understood. I told him what the police officer said about how we didn't raise Carly with morals. He said he and his wife had heard that one before, too. Then he told me about Phil.

He said Phil wasn't always like this. When Phil was a teenager, he was very athletic. He was also funny and kind, and they did everything together.

I cried and told Phil's father similar things about Carly. We talked about how this is the way we see these kids. This is what we remember. The drug addict that other people see is not the same person that we know.

The truth is a gray area. The truth is mixed in with laughter, tears, trauma, rain, snow, and heat. I face the truth about me... that one sentence that I confess to myself and only to myself. I think about other people who have that one sentence that defines them. He robbed a bank. She is a prostitute. He is a heroin addict. But there were thousands of things that took place before that one sentence became their "truth." That doesn't forgive the moment when we jumped the tracks. But it's important to remember what it was like before we made that leap—and to remember there is more to the "truth" about a person than that one statement.

Phil's dad and I talked for another half hour, and for the first time in many years I spoke with someone who really, deeply understood. He and his wife lived our heartbreak every day. Someone understood.

It was like a weight lifted off my shoulders to talk to someone who could truly understand our pain. He decided not to press charges, and told me he wished well for Carly.

I told him with all my heart I hoped Phil came around, and I was so sorry for any additional pain we had caused him and his family. He told us to call if we needed anything. I was so, so grateful for that conversation.

I'll never have a conversation quite like that one again because people really don't get it. They want to, but they just don't.

When you watch an addict, they change. Every time you see them, they are different. Not in a good way. A piece of their goodness is gone. Piece by piece, they become someone else. Every time they use, they are robbed of something precious that makes them who they are. It is stolen and floats away while they are high until they are empty of any trace of the person God brought to the earth. After that, you have to search and dig to find something good in that person. Is the person you used to know still in there somewhere? Or have you lost that person forever? And you mourn the person who used to fill your life with such hope. The person looks different and talks different…the person becomes someone else. So there's a constant feeling of missing someone. The person you knew just isn't there anymore, and all those years of their descent are lost forever. She may recover—you pray she recovers—but she will come out on the other end a different person. You never really get back the person you lost.

The past couple of years we have had Carly away from home in treatment facilities more than we've had her home. So we miss her. But she's different now. Who do we miss?

We miss the girl she was before she started using. She started using as a little twelve-year-old girl. I hardly remember that girl. But sometimes when I look at Carly and she smiles or laughs really hard, I see that little girl again. Just for a second, I remember. And it makes my heart happy.

Michael is John's son. Michael was raised in Chicago by John's first wife and by Michael's stepfather, and John was not permitted to see Michael. I guess Michael's mother felt that the tension between John and Michael's stepfather was so extreme that it was in Michael's best interest for John to move on with his life. John was not happy about this and was very depressed for many, many years.

Michael was John's world. John adored Michael, and could tell stories forever about how amazing Michael was. John would get periodic updates from his sister, who also lived in Chicago, about Michael's baseball career. John would also get newspaper clippings with Michael playing baseball and doing great things. Although John wasn't there to watch all of this, he was so, so proud. Every opportunity John got to show the clippings to someone, you could see the smile and pride in his face. But that would be as close as John would get to Michael for almost twenty years.

MySpace is huge. It's a tool on the web to keep in touch with friends, network, or be stalked by a serial killer. I'm old, but I'm very hip. I have my own MySpace, and I still believe to this day that mine is the best MySpace on the World Wide Web. All the girls have a MySpace as well, which is great because this way I can find out what's going on in their lives by what their pages look like. If they're happy, their pages are happy with happy music. If they're depressed, their pages are depressing with horrible violent music.

I am a social networking enthusiast. I will join every different site so I can be like popular people. In the morning I dress Mom, give her breakfast, and then I check my computer people. I check my MySpace, my Facebook, my Twitter, my Blogger, my Soul Pancake, my Live Journal, my e-mail, my IMs, and then I check my voicemail. I weave in and out of Google. You don't even have to go to college anymore. Recipes? Google it. Heart condition? Google. Herpes? Google. Mental illness? Google. By the time I check all these important things, it's time to get Mom a late lunch.

We tried to find Michael periodically, hoping he would be

living out on his own in Chicago now that he was older. We also thought he might try to find us if we didn't find him. John had last seen Michael when Michael was five years old. Now Michael would be twenty-five. So we "MySpaced" Michael. Nothing.

Then one day, Carly was sitting at the computer when I remembered that Michael had a brother. We had never tried to find the brother, but if we found the brother, we could find Michael. I gave Carly the name, she typed it in, and there he was...the right name, right age, right city...just standing there in the MySpace photo, waiting for Carly to send him a message.

So Carly sent a message, and he responded back confirming that he is Michael's brother. Carly told him that she is Michael's sister, and that she just wanted to say hello to Michael—if Michael was okay with that.

About an hour later, Carly received an e-mail from Michael saying that he got the message from his brother, and that he didn't even know he had a sister.

Carly and Michael talked back and forth on the computer all that day. Then John walked in the door that evening.

I ran to the door and said, "You're not going to believe who Carly is talking to right now! Michael!"

John said, "Michael?" like he didn't know who I was talking about.

I said, "Your son, Michael!"

John looked like he was going to pass out. He walked over to the computer and said, "Are you kidding with me?"

It turned out Michael lived in Las Vegas, which is four hours away from us. We made arrangements for John and Michael to talk on the phone. That first telephone conversation worried me because John is not much of a talker. But they talked and talked like they hadn't been apart for a minute. They talked about their team, the Cubs, and every other sport in the world. When I stood by the window and heard John talking to his son, I was overwhelmed with emotion. John and his son, talking.

The weeks went by, and John talked to Michael almost daily. We made a plan that we would go to Vegas to see Michael, and then he would come back with us for Thanksgiving to meet his brand new sisters and our family, which would be his family, also. Sorry, Michael. You can pick your friends…

The problem was that we had some stuff going on. Carly was back to using all the time again. And unfortunately, so was Andy, who was now officially Carly's boyfriend. Andy's Suboxone was five hundred dollars a month, and when he ran out of money, he relapsed. Jen had a new girlfriend, and April had domestic issues on the horizon. We had waited twenty years to see Michael, and we found him when our lives were in the worst turmoil ever.

So I had to get the family perfect so Michael would accept us. Everything had to be perfect. We had to be the opposite of what we were. We had to be the completely normal family from suburbia, so Michael wouldn't know that we were like the Titanic, two feet from the iceberg. I had two weeks to turn our lives into something amazing so we didn't frighten Michael and make him run away screaming.

It was a huge event that Michael would be at Thanksgiving dinner. John's family, who hadn't seen Michael since he was a baby, would be at dinner as well. I had a small concern about John's sister, Cheryl (aka, "if there is something inappropriate to say I can't stop it from coming out of my mouth"). She would be bringing the sweet potatoes. I felt that I could make my family normal in two weeks, but Cheryl? That was a whole other bowl of cherries.

I bought new dishes, new silverware, napkins with fallish rings to put them in, and a beautiful tablecloth to bring it all together—everything for twenty-six dollars. The dollar store. That's what I had to work with. I placed all the things on the table a week ahead of time to make sure it looked great, and it did. It looked more like fifty dollars. It looked very "normal." How could Michael not accept us when I'm like Martha Stewart?

When the time came, John and I went to Vegas to see Michael. I haven't told you about me and Vegas yet. Vegas is another issue for me. Money is not money in Vegas. It's credits. I could lose every dime we have in forty-five minutes if I am left alone. Regrettably, Vegas isn't something I can address at this second. But I'll get to it as soon as I finish telling negative things about everyone else. Anyway, this time we weren't going to Vegas to gamble. We were going to see John's son.

John and I pulled up to the apartment where Michael lives. We were both nervous wrecks, thinking, What if he hates us?

Just then, a tall, handsome young man walked out. We didn't know what Michael looked like, so we didn't know if it was him or not. Then he smiled, and he looked just like the baby pictures we have all over the house. It was him. He looked just like my husband—ridiculously handsome.

Michael approached us, smiling. John smiled. John was so proud and happy. John hugged Michael. I hugged Michael. Michael got in the front seat and I got in the back, and immediately we all started talking and never stopped. The nerves were gone.

Michael is so amazing—relaxed, a great sense of humor. His mom did an awesome job with him. I adored Michael five minutes after meeting him, and still do. I mean this guy is the coolest young man on the planet.

Thanksgiving Day with Michael was an incredible day. Not perfect, but really, really great. One of the most incredible days I've ever had in my life. Michael blended immediately with everyone, even Cheryl.

With Cheryl, it's black or white. You either love her or hate her, and I think Michael loved her. We spent the day eating and laughing and laughing some more. We took hundreds of pictures of Michael, Jen, April, and Carly. The kids. After it got dark, we had a fire in the outside fireplace, and we sat around it and talked about all the years. Later that night Michael, Jen, and April went out somewhere, and even though I hate the drinking, I loved that they went somewhere together. They came home hours later, and seemed to have had a good time, laughing and talking.

In our household, we seem to always have two extremes happening at the same time. Thanksgiving Day with Michael was great, but we had trouble brewing all day.

That morning, as I stood by the table admiring my work, John walked over to me and whispered in his angry voice, "Carly and Andy are fucking high."

I knew my Martha Stewart Holiday was going to be ruined. Nothing ruins the holiday magic like heroin.

I spent the day trying to send Carly to various rooms so people wouldn't notice that she would be saying something and then, in mid sentence, fall asleep. It was very uncomfortable and embarrassing. It was absolutely not something John or I could address on this particular occasion. We just had to do the best we could. We didn't want to have a domestic on a holiday with a house full of people and a new son.

We had previously been successful at shielding John's family from Carly when she was high. So this was their first time actually seeing her this way. We had told Michael about Carly's condition, but I don't think people really comprehend heroin addiction until it's slouching next to them on the couch.

I walked into the living room, and Carly was sitting on the couch in front of her aunts, uncles, and cousins, sleeping, sitting up. Her eyes rolling back into her head. You couldn't really talk to her about it because she was so high. I'd tell her to go lie down, and she'd lift her head and say she wasn't tired. I'd pull her in the bedroom and tell her to stay there. Thirty seconds later she'd float out and talk to people, not knowing what she was saying, and then fall asleep standing up. It made me sad because I knew this wasn't the real Carly, but Michael didn't know that. This was all he knew about her.

The day before Michael left I was feeling strong, so I decided to talk to him about Carly. I sat on the couch next to Michael and said, "You know, Carly…" and then I started sobbing uncontrollably. I said, "She's such a good person…if you knew her… she's funny and beautiful, and I wish you would just give her a chance…"

Michael looked at me in a really compassionate way and said, "It's okay. There will be many other times that Carly and I will be together. I'm not going anywhere. It's okay." It made me love him even more.

If we are lucky enough to have ten really extraordinary days in our life, that Thanksgiving Day was one of my top ten. We'll never be able to top it. I love that I have three daughters and a brand new son.

In my house, we talk freely about alcohol, heroin, meth, coke, pot, OxyContin, and other drugs. We also talk about sobriety, rehab, hope, God, and faith. We make constant jokes about drugs and alcohol because it takes away the pain of the thing.

John bought some really expensive silverware from Jen because she was selling it as part of her new job, and well, we want her to love us. We spent $380 for silverware to help her out. I told the kids not to use the thirty-five dollar spoons for heroin. That's what the old spoons are for. More morals.

Two of my daughters have boyfriends and one has girlfriends. If you've never had to deal with a daughter's relationships, this is how it works.

Your daughter walks in the front door, crying and holding a suitcase, screaming, "I changed my phone number! I don't ever want to talk to him again!"

I try to comfort her, but then I ask the question, "What happened?" Stupid, stupid thing to ask. Because she tells me.

"First of all, he's a drug dealer! Did you know that?! He's a fucking scumbag! He's high or drunk all the time! That stupid son of a bitch! And you know what else?! I walk in the door the other day and he's wearing my bra and panties! I swear! He runs in the room and slams the door like the little fucking girl he is, and I say, 'What the hell? Why are you wearing my

*underwear?' And the dumb ass is so drunk he says he didn't
know they were mine! He made a mistake and put them on!
And you know what else?! He killed a family of six in Kentucky!
The whole fucking family! He blew them up in their own van!
Then after their van blew up, it careened off the road and hit a
bus filled with nuns and tiny children and that bus drove over a
cliff. A grand total of sixty-seven people dead! Then he drives
off and nobody ever found out it was him! Can you believe this
guy?! And he has the nerve to cheat on me when I have all this
information?! Is he fucking crazy?!"*

The phone rings.

*"Tell him I'm not here! Then tell him to fuck himself and
hang up!"*

*Three days later, it's my birthday. She walks in with Hell Boy.
I pull her aside and say, "Uhm...why is he here?"*

"I love him, Mom, but..."

"But what?"

"Stop trying to run my life, Mother."

"But he..."

"You're not perfect, Mother."

"Yeah, but..."

"Jen's girlfriend calls her a whore all the time."

"But I'm worried..."

"Stop judging."

*Prince Charming walks over with his bouquet of dead flow-
ers, hugs me, and says, "Happy Birthday! What are you now?
Twenty-five!" Hilarious.*

If you want your daughter to get married and have six children with someone you hate, order her not to see that boy again. This makes the boy hotter than ever. Now she has to have this boy, and she will go to any length to see him and be with him just because you said you can't stand the guy.

So now when she walks in the door with some shit sack who is wearing an ankle monitor because the authorities are tracking his movement, you should say, "He's the one!" Tell your daughter you can see they have a terrific chemistry, and say things like, "He's a keeper," and "You shouldn't let that one out of your sight," and "If I were thirty years younger, I'd grab him up myself." She will get this look on her face like she's standing on the side of the highway with a flat tire.

Then when she's not with him, ask why not. Tell her you realize that because of the ankle monitor, his time out is limited, but that she should be on the phone with him when she's not with him. Send him an e-mail or a text message. Just do not let someone else get to him because you already consider him "family."

I guarantee, not only will you never see him again, neither will she.

My heartbreaks are no different from the heartbreaks of other people. The things that break our hearts might be different, but the heartbreaks are the same. Be especially wary when somebody says, "It couldn't get worse than this." Hold on. It could. But it's like the waves in the ocean. They roll in and they roll out. It's good, it's bad. When it's bad, remember that a new wave is coming. It will get good again. You can't stop the wave. It's life.

People don't understand, so you don't say anything. In the darkness, lying in bed at night, you cry into your pillow so you don't wake your spouse. Then you wake up the next day and try to smile so the other family members don't know how broken you are. But then you wonder if they're as broken as you are. Do they cry at night when no one can see them? I bet they do.

Shortly before our Thanksgiving with Michael, my doctor prescribed Klonopin for me for night terrors and anxiety. I took it. It was one week before the anniversary of my six years of sobriety, and because of the prescription, I wasn't considered clean and sober anymore. It was a difficult choice. But I knew better than to completely hurl myself off the cliff and buy a twelve pack of Heineken because that would never end. The Klonopin is a temporary thing until things calm down. I hope that time will be soon.

There are millions of people out there who live this way, and their hearts are breaking just like mine. It's okay to say, "My kid is a drug addict or alcoholic, and I still love them and I'm still proud of them." Hold your head up and have a cappuccino. Take a trip. Hang your Christmas lights and hide colored eggs. Cry, laugh, then take a nap. And when we all get to the end of the road, I'm going to write a story that's so happy it's going to make your liver explode. It's going to be a great day.

God,

The big things in my life are obvious. The kids, the finances, Mom. But I'm trying a new thing of really paying more attention to the little things. Because the little things are what make the big things tolerable.

Each morning I get my cup of coffee. The real treat is when I put my French vanilla creamer in my coffee. It's the first drink that takes you to a whole other emotional place. I enjoy it, standing at the sink filled with dirty dishes, and I smile each time.

The other day I got my car washed. I got the lemon scent. I'm not kidding when I tell you my car smelled like a lemon factory. It was unbelievably gratifying.

What I'm trying to say is that I'm grateful. For all these little things you put in my life that make me smile. The creamer, the smell of lemons from a little cardboard that is shaped like a lemon. I'm grateful for avocados. I'm grateful for hot tea. I'm grateful for Earth, Wind and Fire and James Taylor.

But one thing. Please, God, help John's tooth feel better until we have health insurance. I'm not saying you made a mistake, but what is the purpose of wisdom teeth? We have to pay large sums of money to have them removed. They're like tonsils. It's like you put a whole person together and had parts left over and said, "Just put them in the mouth somewhere."

Anyway, thank you. You lead my life and as of right now I'm really waiting for further direction. Like, I'm actually looking up to you and saying, "Hey! What do I do now?" So I'm sure you're working on something and then I'll get that message. Until then, I'll wait. For a message.

Amen.

Suck My Dick Van Dyke

I had Jennifer's five-year-old birthday party in the park. I woke up that morning with the usual ailments—pounding head, thick throat, still drunk. The night before, I had gone out like I did every night. I worked in a bar so I could get away with this because I'd say I was working, which I was, but at this job, I could drink while I worked—and to me, that was better than medical benefits. Then the employees would all drink until well after the sun came up.

I jump up. I have seven dollars in my pocket. I get ready, brush my teeth three times, but I'm still drunk so the stench is going nowhere. I run out the door and stop at a drug store and find a five-dollar necklace with a little jewel on it.

I get to the park where the party is already in progress. I get a couple of glares from other parents, which I deserve for showing up two hours late to my child's party. I see Jen sitting at a picnic table by herself. I try to act normal and smile, quickly walking toward her. She sees me, starts crying, and puts her head on her arms on the table. I sit next to her and pretend I don't know why she is crying. I try to hug her but she pushes me away. I tell her I brought her something and pull the five-dollar necklace out of my purse. My hands are shaking from the booze trying to escape my body.

I set the necklace by her elbow. She looks up and says, "I didn't think you were coming to my party!" Then she puts her head back down, still crying, and pushes the necklace across the table with her elbow.

I feel disgusted with myself. Sick to my stomach. We sit in silence for a few minutes. I say, "Come here. Sit on my lap." So I pick her up and put her on my lap. I hug her and kiss her, and she melts into my arms sniffling and crying.

Her tears begin to subside. I tell her I bought the necklace especially for her and then I hand it back to her. She stays curled up in a ball in my arms looking at the necklace. With red eyes and a wet face, she smiles and says, "It has a jewel on it."

I say, "That's because you're a princess." I put the necklace around her neck, and she jumps off my lap and runs over to show her necklace to the other children.

I only drank for another twenty years. There are so many stories that haunt me, like Jen's five-year-old birthday party. Images that don't go away. Events that were supposed to be happy, but in the end gave me and the kids nightmares. I know I can never fix those memories, or erase them, or regain the time that was lost.

———— ❧ ————

A week before I had Jennifer, I went to the Goodwill to get a crib. I also found a baby t-shirt that said "I'm spoiled" across the front. I returned to my parents' house with the only crib I could afford. It had all the pieces, but it didn't come with any screws to keep it together, so I tied it with rope in thirty different places. You could push the crib with one finger and it would rock back and forth as if it were going to fall to the floor. But I thought it was suitable for a tiny baby that didn't weigh very much.

I recall bringing Jennifer home and laying her in that death trap with her little "I'm spoiled" t-shirt and I think, Yes…perfect…a six pound human in a crib that may crash to the ground any second, but maybe not. We'll see. Knock wood.

I did so well with the first child, living with my parents, on food stamps and welfare, that I was pregnant with my second daughter at nineteen.

My job back then was a paper route. I used my father's green VW van to deliver the papers. Jennifer was two years old, and she played in the back of the van as I threw the paper route. When I would turn a corner I could hear her roll and hit the wall of the van. This is the kind of mother I was. She acted like it was nothing. She just sat up and continued playing.

I'm nine-and-a-half months pregnant, and I'm rolling the papers as I drive, throwing them here and there. I have a contraction. I don't think much of it. I continue on, wrapping papers, throwing papers. A short time later, another contraction. I step on the pedal.

No one knows my route but me, so I have to finish it before I go to the hospital because this paper route is my career. It's a lot of pressure for a huge pregnant teen with a two-year-old slamming into the walls in the back of the van. But if I do a good job, I can throw these papers until I am dead.

It is a four hour paper route, so I speed up, feeling a bit nervous. I hear Jen hitting the walls as I speed up and turn faster. More contractions and they're getting closer together so I stop and pick up my mother.

I run in the house holding the bottom of my stomach as if the baby would actually fall out.

I tell my mom, "I'm having the baby! You have to drive! Hurry!" We run out and jump in the van.

I direct her and tell her, "Mother! Drive faster!" She drives faster and the contractions are closer and longer. I'm throwing papers like a wild person. I don't know if I'm throwing them at the right houses but I think, fuck it. They get one, they get one, they get one. We speed through the dirt roads for three hours and we're almost done when my water breaks. We finish the paper route at three o'clock, go back by the house to pick up my little overnight bag, and then finally go to the hospital. April is born at six thirty.

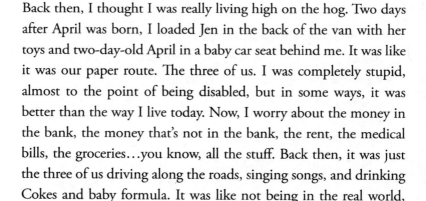

Back then, I thought I was really living high on the hog. Two days after April was born, I loaded Jen in the back of the van with her toys and two-day-old April in a baby car seat behind me. It was like it was our paper route. The three of us. I was completely stupid, almost to the point of being disabled, but in some ways, it was better than the way I live today. Now, I worry about the money in the bank, the money that's not in the bank, the rent, the medical bills, the groceries…you know, all the stuff. Back then, it was just the three of us driving along the roads, singing songs, and drinking Cokes and baby formula. It was like not being in the real world, and there's nothing wrong with that.

I had Jennifer when I was eighteen, got married when I was nineteen, had April when I was twenty, got divorced when I was twenty-one, and then slept in my car with my girls for a while after the divorce. We only slept in the car for two weeks, but it seemed like longer. Then we stayed with family and friends… floating around from day-to-day, staying at different places.

'Nuff said about my first marriage. I'm sure there were some real interesting things that happened, they just don't ever come to mind—and the things that do come to mind, I'm treating with powerful antidepressants.

Then I married John and we had Carly. During the first twelve years of our marriage, I drank until I stumbled to bed, and John smoked pot until all the snacks in the house were gone.

Every night at seven thirty I would open my first beer. I preferred Heineken, but when times were bad I would choke back Rolling Rock. At about the same time each night, John would have to "go do things in the garage." He'd walk back in the house happy with red watery eyes. This is how we lived for so, so long. I guess the girls thought it was just normal. They had friends whose parents were doing the same things or worse. All the parents had the same excuses. We were under stress, or had a bad day, or it was seven thirty.

Toward the end of my twenty-something years of drinking, I began to get really mean when I drank. I would pick a screaming fight with John every night. John, high on pot, couldn't defend himself because he was confused and couldn't string together an entire sentence. So I screamed like a crazy person. The girls would sit in their bedrooms and listen to all of it. Sometimes it would go on most of the night. Or at least until the Heineken was gone.

John would say the slightest thing like, "Did we pay the phone bill?"

I'd slur, "Good God, fuck off."

One night I told John to "Suck my big fat cock." The next day he told me he couldn't believe I had said that to him. I quickly lied and said, "I didn't say, 'Suck my big fat cock.' (Long pause so I could think.) I said, 'Suck my Dick Van Dyke.'" I told him I said it to be funny. A big fat lie, but one of the best lies I've ever told. Suck my Dick Van Dyke? What does that even mean?

I would scream things like that all night. I know now the damage it caused to all three of our girls. I wish I could erase it, but I can't. I was a lunatic. The girls started getting into trouble, and I would stagger to their rooms and slur my warnings about how alcohol problems run in our family. Of course, this didn't include me because I went to work every day and I waited until seven thirty to drink. But those other people were definitely alcoholics. I'd say, "Alcoholismrunsinthefamily" (everything is one word when you're drunk). The way the words came out of my mouth, it sounded like my tongue was swollen. The girls just stared at me and didn't respond.

And they didn't take my advice. They were teenagers, and they were drinking and using drugs regularly—just like their parents.

So I would lecture them some more, holding onto the door the whole time so I wouldn't fall on the floor, thinking I was saying something really meaningful. Then I would throw in something random like, "Wherearemyshoes?"

They'd say, "One of them is under the computer desk because you threw it at John."

Jen raised herself into becoming a teenager and began running wild like nothing I'd ever seen before. She would just leave and not come back for days. We would look everywhere for her. I was having panic attacks and night terrors. I would wake up suddenly in the middle of the night and be filled with terror, with my heart racing. Then I couldn't go back to sleep. I would lie in my bed wondering where she was and if we would get a phone call saying something happened to her.

So just for kicks, one night I said a prayer, which is something I hadn't done for many, many years. I asked God to watch over Jen since she wouldn't allow us to watch over her. I prayed for sleep without night terrors. I said that if I could have one night's sleep I would be ready for whatever comes tomorrow. I was just so tired.

Please God, can I have one night without waking up in terror?

I woke up the next morning and walked into the living room. It was sort of dark outside. John asked if I was sick. I said I wasn't. He said that they had been trying to wake me all day but I wouldn't get up. I had fallen asleep the night before and hadn't woken up until the following evening. Then I remembered my prayer telling God I was tired. I looked over and Jen was sitting on the couch watching TV. That's when I started to believe in God again. I started to believe that someone was watching over me.

—————◦⧓◦—————

I attempted sobriety three times before I had any success. The first time, I went to one of the stupid meetings. These crazy people would go up there and say things like, "I crashed into a car and killed seven people." Or "I left my two-year-old at a bus stop."

I was sitting there thinking, "I'm not like these people. These people are crazy. I'm not crazy. I'm just sad. And thirsty."

Five days in, I asked my alcoholic friends and family if they thought I was an alcoholic. They took a sip of their wine and said,

"You are so not an alcoholic." See, you just have to know the right people to ask.

The second time I tried sobriety was when we lived in Las Vegas. Same deal. I listened to the crazies and thought, I'm not like these people.

When people talk about their "bottom," it's sometimes this really horrible thing that happened. But there are people like me who didn't have that one big event.

For me, it was a gradual thing. I felt empty and sad for years, and for a long, long time, alcohol worked. I'd drink, and all the sadness would go away. Not only did the sadness go away, but I was fantastic. I was beautiful, funny, I had a great figure, and I could do math.

But at some point, the booze stopped working. That's when drinking started sucking. Every time I drank, I could feel pieces of me leaving. I continued to drink until there was nothing left. Just emptiness. If someone had screamed and I had my mouth open, it would have echoed.

The third time I tried to quit drinking was after we were back in Phoenix. I went to bed drunk one night like I always did. Moses was seven months old, and April was having a really difficult time with the reality of his condition. Moses was on several different seizure medications.

Jen was just gone. The alcohol, drugs, cutting, craziness.

I said a prayer that night asking God to help me find a way to help the girls. I just didn't know what to do for them. The alcohol made me more depressed, so I would sit on the couch and cry and drink one after another. Cry, drink, throw things at John.

The next morning I woke up and the first thought I had was that I was going back to the meetings with the crazy people.

I got there and I couldn't get in because it was too crowded. So I sat outside and talked to a crazy person. He was a recovering alcoholic, and we talked and laughed. I was leaving and he said, "Just for tonight, don't drink."

I went home and I thought, Just for tonight I'm not drinking. I began having panic attacks in the middle of the night. The second night I decided not to drink one more night. The second night was really bad. The panic was overwhelming. My body tingled (in a bad way) from the top of my head to my toes. My skin itched. My head was pounding. I went back to the meeting the next day. I listened to crazy people and thought, "What a drag. I'm exactly like these people."

Days went by, weeks went by, meetings and meetings. I made great friendships and had more laughs than I have ever had in my life. Months went by and then years went by.

For the first thirty days of my sobriety, I had a migraine that never went away. Some days I would throw up. It was ugly but so worth pushing through to the other side.

What's on the other side? The exact same bullshit. But now I can at least deal with it—and what I can't deal with, I can laugh about. You have nothing to cushion the blow of life. All you can do is laugh. You've been robbing Peter to pay Paul and then there's a knock on your door. Guess who it is? Peter. He wants his fucking money. All you can do is laugh.

If you use drugs or alcohol, your kids will also use. Your kids do what you do, and in my life that's very scary. If you're following in my footsteps, wear a helmet.

John and I fought for years, and I know this is a big part of what is going on with the girls. Our drug and alcohol use is another big part. I stopped drinking and John quit smoking pot around the same time. It's hardly a coincidence that our fighting, other than normal you-annoy-me fighting, completely stopped when we stopped our seven thirty routine. Our whole life changed. We began to treat each other with more respect. I stopped throwing shoes at him. For the most part. There are still times when nothing says it like a Nike to the back of the head.

When you drink too much you lose things. Car keys, your purse, money, kids. It comes with the territory. Every alcoholic has lost her car at least once. You wake up in the morning and you look out the window and say, "Hey. Where's my car?"

Losing a car is not unusual for an alcoholic, so you call friends and try to find your car. I called a friend, and she said I gave my car away at a house party. What? She said I went out to my car, came back in with the title and signed it away to some stranger. I said I would never do such a thing. She said she tried to stop me, but I told her the guy was real sweet and he was having trouble getting back and forth to school. Apparently it was more important that the stranger got to school than it was for me to care for my two small daughters as a single mom. At the end of the party I actually had to find a ride home.

People have asked me what the difference is between just "having a good time" and actually being an alcoholic.

Most people at happy hour are having a good time. But some of those people go home and pee on their floor. That's an indication there may be a problem.

Regular having-a-good-time people don't wake up in a pool

of vomit. If you have been cut off in a bar, that could be a problem. If you don't remember the night before and you wake up with random injuries on your body and leaves and sticks in your hair, could be an issue. If you get drunk, call every person you know, tell them you're going to kill yourself, and then wake up the next day and decide to join a gym, something is very wrong. If you think everyone in the world is against you and you are completely mistreated…if you think your drinking only affects you… if you drink because your life sucks more than anyone else's…if you drink because all the people around you are fuckers…and the biggest one, if you've ever asked yourself, "Am I an alcoholic?"… God bless you, you are probably an alcoholic.

Here are some other ways to figure out if you're an alcoholic or addict.

If a sign says, "Take One," alcoholics and addicts always take four. They always park in handicapped parking spaces and fire lanes. They always have sixty-five items in the express lane. They don't let people merge on the highway. If their eyes are brown, they say they're blue. They have a sweet collection of shot glasses, but their children don't have diapers. They stack empty beer cans in the built-in bookcase to look like the Egyptian pyramids, but they don't have a single book. They challenge walls to a fist fight and lose. If any of this sounds like you at all, cut people off all the way to detox. And make a mental note: the wall always wins.

If someone said to you, "If you use drugs, you will lose your family, your job, all your money and your dignity, but your legs will feel like pudding," what would you say? A normal person doesn't even think twice about this choice. But addicts and alcoholics could go back and forth for hours: "My family? Pudding? All of my money? Pudding? Hmmm. What do I do?" Most of the people I know would choose the pudding. So at the end of the day, there we are, with legs that feel like pudding.

I know my brain is wired for pudding, so I have to focus on everything I do or I will end up living behind a dumpster. For me it could happen so easily.

I would go see my pharmacist "Julio" at his office, which is located on a sidewalk downtown. I'd try using some small talk with him: "Hi, Julio. How's your family?"

Julio would just get angry. "Give me the money, I'll give you the pills, and then you walk away. Don't fucking talk to me."

Drug dealers have zero customer service skills. Their PSS is about 20.

Drug addiction is only funny if you're a drug addict or alcoholic. It's like when you're a member of a particular ethnic group, you can say funny things about that ethnic group. It's the same with addicts and alcoholics.

I have a friend who said to one of my family members, "Hey! I hardly recognized you without the ski mask!" This family member got an idea one night, when his legs were like pudding. He went to the grocery store, got a bottle of expensive vodka, put a ski mask on and ran out. He could have been shot, but he thought it was a good idea.

I eventually got my car back, but do you know how I got to that place of giving my car away at a house party? Pudding. All the chaos and bullshit in the entire world begins with people who have legs that feel like pudding.

Losing your car is not the worst thing that can happen when you drink. Sometimes when you drink too much, you lose one of your kids. I don't mean they get taken away, although that happens, too. I mean, "I can't find my kid. There was a four-year-old right here, and now, where is that kid?"

When Jen was two years old, I brought April home from the hospital. April was two days old.

Jen said, "Where'd you get that baby?"

I said, "She's our baby now! Isn't she cute?"

Jen said, "Yeah. Well. You could take her back if you want."

I said, "Actually, Sweetie, she's your little sister! You have to help with her and be very gentle!"

Jen: "Can I go play now?"

Two weeks later, I was in the kitchen where there was a big window looking out on the back yard. I could see little Jen playing on a worm toy that you sit on and it rolls. April was sleeping.

I continue what I'm doing, going from room to room doing various things with a cigarette in my hand at all times. I walk by the back window, and I see the worm toy but no Jen. I go out the back door and yell, "Jennifer!" I walk around the outside of the house. No Jen. I go back in the house. No Jen. Now I'm panicked.

I wake up my father—because, of course, I live with my parents. He jumps up to help, but we can't find her. Our house is on a two acre piece of land, and the houses are separated by big plots of land. There is our house, the neighbor's house and then a huge ditch. My dad looks down the dirt road toward the ditch and says, "Stay here." He later tells me that he didn't want me there if he found her in the ditch.

So I'm still looking for Jen on the land by our house, looking up the road. Nothing. No Jen. My father comes back and says he couldn't find her. We call the police, and they say they got a call from a person who saw a little girl walking down the street with two dogs. He picked her up and took her and the dogs to his house.

It turns out the young man who picked Jen up is a popular boxer in Albuquerque. He has a big, pretty house. We pull up, and Jen is having the time of her life playing on the swing set with several other children. I run up to her and grab her and hug her. I say, "You cannot ever go for a walk alone! Ever!"

She says, "I wasn't alone. I was with the dogs."

We thank the boxer—thank God for him. We're driving home and I say, "Jennifer, you cannot ever do that again!"

She says, "Okay" and looks out the window. Then she looks at me and says, "So you still have that baby?"

I also lost Carly. I was in the kitchen again. I seem to lose children when I go in the kitchen.

Carly is three. She walks into the kitchen, and she is wearing hot pink sweat pants, those plastic high heels covered with shiny jewels you get from Kmart, no shirt, a necklace, and a ton of my makeup on her eyelids and lips. She looks like a three-year-old stripper. She's holding her plastic pink purse and pushing her Fisher Price plastic shopping cart.

She says to me, "I'm going shopping now."

I say, "Okay! Get me some bread and some dish soap!"

About ten minutes later I notice how quiet it is. I yell,

"Carly!" No answer. I walk around the house. No Carly. I look out the front window and see that the screen to the window is kicked out and the front wood gate is open. I run out the front door. I look both ways up and down the street. Nothing. So I just start to run in the direction of the closest busy street.

I'm running and I see a Hispanic lady standing on the street. As I run by she says in a very thick Hispanic accent, "There's a baby, just walking down that street."

I run the direction she points. I come around the corner where the elementary school is and look up the street. On the corner of the busy street is Carly with her high heels and shopping cart, and a lady leaning over talking to her. I run to the corner. I get there completely out of breath and say to the lady, "Thank God you saw her."

The lady said she worked at the school and was teaching her class when she saw Carly come around the corner. The woman didn't see any adults with Carly, so she left her classroom, followed Carly, and then stopped her at the busy street.

The first thing Carly said to the teacher was, "Can you cross me? I'm not allowed to step off the curb."

The teacher said, "Where is your mother?"

Carly told her, "My mother sent me to get bread and soap."

That's when I got there.

I should have known we would have problems when a three-year-old could kick out a screen window with plastic pink pumps.

To my credit, I never lost April. Not once.

When Carly was two, my father died of cancer. By the time they found the cancer, it had spread throughout his body. They checked him into the hospital and told him he could have a surgery that would prolong his life for about two weeks, or he could skip the surgery and they would do their best to make him comfortable. All of us adult kids and Mom were standing around his bed. Dad decided he didn't want the surgery. All his organs were shutting down, and two weeks would just add more pain.

The hospital began giving Dad morphine. He was groggy for a few days. Then they began giving him huge doses of morphine. After that he fell asleep and never really did wake up, but he lived another eight days. So for eight days, all six of us kids and my mother sat around Dad's bed, watching him sleep.

When my father got sick, we tried the loud desperate praying, but he inevitably ended up in the hospital. Right before my father died, he called each of his children into his hospital room, I guess to say something meaningful.

Each sibling came out crying and said something like, "He said he was proud of me."

Then the next one: "He said he loved me and he was proud I was his son!"

The next one: "He said he loved me and he wanted me to be happy in my life!"

Then me. I walked in and leaned next to him and waited for something really great. He whispered, "Watch out for the little guy."

What? Watch out for the little guy? What does that mean?

I walked out and the group was looking at me. I wasn't crying. I said, "Dad said for me to watch out for the little guy."

Silence. My brother looked down and started shuffling his feet.

Watch out for the little guy? Really? Are you kidding?

———— ◦◦◦◦ ————

My siblings and I are close, but not so close that we can sit in a tiny room with our comatose father for eight days. We all have separate lives and children, and see each other when we can, but not often. My sister, Lisa, is a take-control kind of person. She spent eight days taking care of Dad's blankets and socks, and fixing pillows, and most of all, calling the nurses nonstop. She'd say, "He needs this or that. What about this? Can you fix that?" This went on all day and night. Call the nurse, call the nurse.

So we began to make jokes about it. Lisa got agitated. We took more breaks outside because she had things under control. We wanted to help somehow, but we couldn't. Lisa was fixing and fluffing and pushing the nurse button. This was how Lisa got through it, and actually, she's always been this way. She is an organizer, a manager. If you want something done, call Lisa.

And in the end, we were all thankful that Lisa was Lisa. We didn't really want to fluff the pillows or change Dad's socks. So mostly we sat. We looked at the floor. Had some small talk. Dad would move and we would all quickly look at him. Then nothing. Then he stopped moving.

Five days in, we got comfortable with Dad lying in the middle of the room in a coma. One brother threw a wadded up piece of paper at another brother right over Dad's comatose body. The victim responded by wadding up a bigger piece of paper and launching it full speed at the other brother, and almost knocked his eye out.

"Christ, you idiot," said my brother. "You hit me in the eye. Lisa, I need some medical attention."

We all tried not to laugh, which caused us to laugh hysterically, even Mom.

We talked about holidays and funny things that had happened over the years. We'd laugh and the nurse would come and scold us for being too rowdy. She'd leave and we'd laugh again. We'd go to lunch and bring back food for Lisa and Mom. I'd go up and down the elevator millions of times so me and my brothers could smoke.

We sat in that room for so long that when we walked outside, the sun hurt our eyes. Every now and then, someone would just start crying. We would comfort that person and take the elevator down to smoke again. An hour or so later, another sibling would start crying, or Mom would start crying. At one point, we were all crying. Just quiet tears rolling down our faces.

Carly was a baby so I went home at night to sleep. One morning, Lisa called and said Dad had passed away.

It was weird. I didn't really feel anything about it. I jumped up and went to the hospital to be with my mom and my brothers and sister.

We all walked out of the hospital and stood quietly on the sidewalk as if we didn't know what to do next. It was a sunny day. For us the world had stopped just for a moment. Nothing was different, yet everything was different. But it was as if the rest of the world had already moved on. People were rushing by with briefcases…people were sitting on the grass…a guy was playing with his dog.

We were all wondering what we could have said or should have said…wishing Dad would have said a particular thing. You have your dad your whole life, and then you don't. It's a very strange feeling.

I can see my mom standing there staring out at the world, looking lost. Her husband of thirty-eight years no longer here. It was just the oddest feeling. As if it wasn't real. My mom shook her head, stepped off the curb, and then walked to her car holding a plastic bag with my father's jeans and shirt neatly folded inside.

She went back to work for financial reasons five days after my father died. But for months, my brother, Patrick, said Mom would lie in her bed at night and cry herself to sleep. Then wake up the next day and smile, get dressed, and take the bus to work.

My father watched me drink my way through life as an active alcoholic for ten years before he died, and never said anything about it to me. I've often wondered why he didn't say something. Like, "I know of Alcoholics Anonymous and you might think about going there." Or "I think your drinking is making your life difficult." Or "Hey, you drunk fuck." Why didn't he say something?

All three of my daughters have said they can't stand it when I give them "input" on their lives. They say they know I'm going to butt into their lives when I say, "May I make a suggestion?" They say that means that if they don't take my suggestion, I'll continue to "suggest" it until they do. I like to see it as me reaching my hand out and feeling comfortable with them getting angry with me. I can take the heat. We may be at dinner and I'll say, "You should go to rehab. Can you pass me the mustard?"

When Carly was twelve, we lived in a very affluent part of Phoenix, but we were the designated poor people. I had started my job as a checker at the grocery store, and John installed flooring.

Carly was just beginning her descent into hell. One day, the mall security called me and said I had to come and pick Carly up because she got caught smoking. Cigarettes.

I picked her up and we were driving home. I said to her, "You know, every day I hear stories about other people's kids. They're playing hockey, or they're honor students, or they're in the school play. When am I going to get to tell a story?"

Carly looked at me and said, "Yeah, that's sort of like how I hear stories from other kids at my school. They talk about their father the doctor or their mother the lawyer. I guess neither of us has a story to tell."

I was silent. My first thought was, Just backhand her. Surprise her with a powerful backhand. There's your story. Then I thought, Wow, she is so smart. She should be a lawyer.

Time out is for little kids, and tough love is for older kids.

When my girls were little, "time out" meant the time it took me to get to you. Go ahead and take that time to relax. Take a breather. But by the time I get to you, the entire situation better have taken a dramatic change for the better.

When my girls were older, "tough love" meant that when you were on crystal meth, I would hang you upside down and shake my money out of your pocket.

Tough love is different for rich people and poor people. For rich people, tough love means taking something away from your kid. That doesn't work for poor people. There is nothing to take away.

I come from generation after generation of poor people.

There are no stories of Great Uncle Whatever doing great things. If you needed twenty bucks, you couldn't get it from Cousin Bob because he lived in a box behind a Kmart. So the kids that made up the branches of my family tree knew ahead of time, you will not get an education past high school. At least not from your parents. You will not get a car at graduation. You will not go to a rehab in the mountains with a stream running through it. You will be sent off into the world with a new pair of jeans and a Snickers bar. Good luck, kid. The world is your oyster.

At the same time, I acknowledge that it is possible to do it all on your own, and many people in my family have. Two of my brothers graduated from college and paid for it themselves while working full time to pay rent, car payments and take care of their families. But they knew ahead of time that's the way it had to happen or it wasn't going to happen. I knew the same thing, but I made different choices. My choices were babies and pudding, not necessarily in that order.

As a result, if one of my kids became a drug addict, I had nothing to dangle in front of her as an incentive to quit. I couldn't say to Carly, "Stop using drugs or I won't pay for your college or your apartment or your car." The only thing I could say was, "Don't use drugs because you'll die." How lame is that? That doesn't work. I could punish her by taking something away from her, but I have never given Carly anything I could take back as a punishment—and yes, that's my own fault. But if I hadn't made the shitty choices I've made, this book would be called, My Sweet Life Will Rock Your World. In the end, the consequences of using drugs are less complicated for poor people. If you use, you die. Period.

During one of her breakups from Andy, Carly was getting drugs from an older crowd of men who had just gotten out of prison. The men were also skinheads. Those were the darkest days of my entire life.

The men had several teenage girls coming in and out of their meth house. The young girls prostituted and gave the money to the men for drugs.

One of the older men gave Carly large amounts of meth in a syringe. Carly said it was too much. He said it wasn't, gave it to her, and then raped her while she was high. Carly was so high, she didn't even remember being raped. She found out about it later, by accident.

> Carly is sitting in a room at the meth house, shooting up. While the drugs are kicking in, something strange happens: she hears her own voice coming from the next room.
>
> She is high and confused, so she thinks maybe she is hearing wrong. She goes to the door to investigate. She finds that it really is her voice. It's coming from a video. The video is a recording of the skinhead drug-dealer ex-con raping Carly after he's drugged her. The skinhead rapist is showing the video to one of the other fuck bags.
>
> In the video, Carly's voice says, "I don't want to."
>
> The skinhead says, "Are we going to do this the hard way?"
>
> Carly says, "I'm only seventeen."
>
> Then the man rapes her.

My fear for Carly while she was around these men was completely suffocating. This was different than Phil. Phil was trying to be a big-shot drug dealer, but he didn't really have a clue. The skinhead ex-cons were long-time, hard-core violent criminals. And Carly was only seventeen. But we didn't know where the men lived, and Carly wouldn't answer her phone.

Something about this change in Carly took a piece out of my heart. Every day watching Carly become someone I didn't know anymore…this was like a final confirmation that this girl wasn't our daughter anymore. She was someone else. There was nothing left of Carly. It felt like a death. I was shattered. I have never in my life been so consumed with sadness.

Carly has been gone for more than a week. I go to the bookstore because I am trying to act normal even though all I can think about is Carly and what she is doing and who she is doing it with.

I get home and John is sitting on the computer, also trying to distract himself. I lay my book on the counter and then suddenly, I break down and start screaming and crying, "Where is she! I want her home!"

John comes over to me and tries to console me. I'm grabbing his shirt, "You have to go find her! Bring my daughter home! I want her home!" I fall on the floor sobbing. "Go get her! I just want my daughter! Please, John, find her! Please! I'm begging you! Go find her! I want her back! Please!" Now John is crying, too.

He leads me to the bedroom so I can lie down, but I keep saying, "You have to go get her! Please, bring her home!" I lie on the bed crying, "Please God, bring her home! Please help us! I want my daughter! Please, God, please!"

John and I cry ourselves to sleep. The whole time I'm mumbling, "I want my daughter back. Please, someone, find her. Please."

The next morning, we could hardly get out of bed. John and I lay there looking at the ceiling, silent. Mom was ringing her bell, waiting to be serviced.

We stumbled through that day the best we could. Mostly lying on the couch, clicking through all two hundred channels over and over again. Sniffling through our tears and not saying anything to each other.

That night we got a phone call from Carly. She said she was at a convenience store and that she was hiding from people, but she didn't know exactly where she was. She put an employee from the store on the phone, and the employee told John how to get there.

The store was an hour from us but only five minutes from John's sister, Cheryl. So John called Cheryl and told her to go get Carly. Five minutes later, Cheryl pulled up to the store, screeching into the parking lot in her hot Mustang. Later, we got the full story.

Carly is at a little store in our area and she's trying to find a ride home. But she doesn't call us. Instead, she accepts a ride from a Hispanic man. An employee at the store says he knows the man, and that the man will give her a ride home.

Carly and the Hispanic man walk to the car. He puts a thirty pack of Bud Light in the back seat, Carly puts her bag in the trunk, and they drive off.

The man gives Carly a bag of cocaine, so she sits on the floor of the car, doing lines off the seat. When she gets up, she realizes they are on the highway.

Carly points in the other direction and tells the man he is going the wrong way. The man says things in Spanish and something about the cocaine.

Carly says, "Just let me out." But the man doesn't stop.

They drive for about forty-five minutes to the other side of town. Carly realizes she has made a huge mistake. Nothing is free.

The man drives Carly into a long alley, and every time she tries to jump out he grabs her arm. He finally comes to the end of the alley where another really big man is waiting. The man walks toward the car, smiling. Carly makes a run for it now that the car is stopped. The first man tries to stop her and pulls her earring out of her ear. Carly jumps out of the car and runs as fast as she can down the long alley. The men jump into their car and drive behind her.

Carly keeps running until she gets to a store. She tells the store clerk what happened, and then she hides because she's afraid the men will come looking for her. The clerk is kind and says she will keep Carly safe. Carly calls us, and John's sister goes to the store to get Carly. The next day, Carly goes into detox. Again.

<hr />

During this time, I became obsessed with learning about drugs. I was reading books and literature and information on the Internet about drugs and addiction, day after day after day.

I did this for a year. Most of the time I felt like I couldn't breathe, but I didn't know why. I wasn't booking any comedy jobs because I didn't feel funny. All the information I was putting in my head was heartbreaking. It was drugs, drugs, death, heartbreak, drugs, drugs, drugs.

After dropping Carly off at yet another rehab, I was officially done. I didn't want to talk or hear or read about drugs anymore. I got rid of all the books and information that had to do with drugs and addiction, and as a result, I suddenly felt very free, like a weight lifted off my shoulders or like I had taken a hot bath. It wasn't up to me anymore. Of course, the rational part of my brain knew all along that I could not fix things for Carly. But that didn't stop me from trying. I finally realized that the only person I am responsible for is me—and most days that's a huge task in itself.

I have had panic attacks since I was a kid. At one point in my life the panic was so bad I didn't leave my house. I had a constant feeling that I was suffocating.

I couldn't go to a drive-through window because if a car got behind me, I would hyperventilate because I felt trapped. I only went to the grocery store at six in the morning or eleven at night because again, if someone got in line behind me, I felt like I couldn't escape. Many times, I just bolted out the door leaving my groceries.

If someone opened the front door when I was at home, I felt like I couldn't breathe. If I was left alone, I would spiral off into a full-blown panic attack. I didn't go anywhere, I didn't do anything. I didn't drive on the highway for ten years. Back streets were also off limits because they frightened me. At one point,

when I was feeling better, I booked a trip to go overseas and per-
form for the troops as a comic. I ended up canceling the trip. In
fact, I canceled any comedy job that required me to travel. I just
sat in my apartment, drinking, for years.

I remember praying every night that God would take my
fear away. I was very limited as to where I could go outside of
my home, and the only time the fear left me was when I had a
few drinks.

Then I stopped drinking and went on an antidepressant. It
was the most amazing thing I could have done to get rid of my
panic. I was almost normal. I could drive on the freeway and flip
people off like a normal person. No anxiety at all.

Everything went like that for years. Then came Carly's overdoses, April's boyfriends, more of Carly's overdoses...trying to
work and smile because it's part of my uniform...taking care of
Mom and Moses and juggle it all. That's when I started taking
the Klonopin.

In the midst of the carnage, April told me I needed to get away,
and that she and her girlfriend were going to Vegas. Yay Vegas!
They wanted me to be their designated driver, and as I soon
found out, they were going to begin partying in the car. Not
ideal, but hey, I'm going to Vegas.

Vegas, baby. I love it. John and I go two or three times a year.
He will only allow us to go for one night.

You will not see a happier me than when I can harass John
into taking me to Vegas. I am all over him until he actually gets
in the car to take me. I mean for weeks I won't let it go. We get in
the car moments before he has a complete mental collapse. Then

I smile and sing the whole way.

When we do go, John has me on a very short leash. He keeps all the credit cards and cash. I have to ask him for money, and I hate it—but I'm in Vegas! John says we have "X" amount of dollars. That's it. I hate that. And trust me, he will not go over that exact amount. If John says we have twelve dollars to spend, he will not spend thirteen, no matter what I say.

> *I say, "I can double our car payment!"*
> *John says, "You're ridiculous."*
> *"No I can! I can double our rent!"*
> *"Come with me. Keep walking."*
> *"I really can. I have a system!"*
> *"Don't stop walking. We're going up to the room."*
> *We go up to the room, and I harass John until we fall asleep.*
> *The next morning, I steal a pillow and then we go home.*
> *John watches me steal the pillow and says, "Why are you doing that?"*
> *I say, "What? I paid for it."*

Vegas is just fun. That's all there is to it. Vegas is the complete opposite of John's and my real life at home.

Now that Michael is there I harass John into the ground even more about going.

> *I say, "Wow. I really miss Michael. Don't you?"*
> *John stares at me. "We're not going to Vegas."*
> *"But…Michael probably misses you, too!"*

"Dina. Stop. We're not going."
"I could double our…"
"Jesus Christ."

I play slot machines. I don't like to talk. If I have the misfortune of sitting next to a talker, I have to move. I just sit and stare at all the little things spinning around. I focus.

The phrase I use most in Vegas is, "Give me twenty bucks." John says I'm like a recording. Another popular phrase is, "I was up." Although I say that much less than I say, "Give me twenty bucks."

We go for the one night, and then in the morning John has to hog tie me and pull me out as I'm screaming, "I can double our electric bill!" Then we do it again in three or four months.

So I am April's escort to Vegas. I am going to Vegas to double the amount of highlights I can put in my hair.

We're in the hotel room. It's ten o'clock at night and the girls are going out. I suddenly begin to have a panic attack. I have no idea why but I'm freaking out. I feel like I can't stay in the hotel room alone, but I can't go with them because I'm old and they're going "clubbing."

I explain this to April. She says, "Don't worry about it. I have a painkiller. It will make you feel better."

I have never taken a painkiller, but I am having a heart attack. I grab it and take it fast.

Ten minutes later, I am not only feeling no pain, but it is the happiest day of my life. I am mumbling and helping them dress, and I am happier than, as they say, a pig in shit. Twenty minutes later, I am sound asleep.

So, like any normal person, I take the pain pills every day for a month after that—just in case I may get some pain later. I take the Klonopin with it. April runs out of the pain pills, and the best thing I can get is Xanax, which is an even happier drug than the pain pills. I now understand crazy Grandma: "Make me my biscuits!"

I'm taking everything I can get my hands on, and I do this for three months when it dawns on me that I'm out of my mind. It has to stop.

So I stop. I go back to my old self, and thank God I didn't go completely off the deep end where I couldn't come back.

How could it be possible to have so much fake happiness in one little tiny pill? It is so easy for me to see how people become addicted. I completely understand. The greatest thing a pharmacist can say to me is, "Don't drive or operate heavy machinery after you take this." I nod my head because my day just got better.

The Klonopin makes me a little tired. The Rolling Rock makes me break things and say "fuck off" to people I love. The pain pills make me so happy it has to be wrong.

Ever since I can remember I've been trying to take the edge off. I bet I was a seven-month-old baby standing in my crib, holding the bars thinking, This is stressful.

Have you noticed how I make all my addictions sound funny? They're not funny, but that's how I deal with it. If you have a better way to deal with it, you should write a book, too.

This is how it feels. You are in second grade. You do all right with your grades, and you get along with your classmates. People see you and think "cute little girl," and your parents think you are the most beautiful person alive. But something is wrong. You're little so you don't understand. But you can feel that you are not like the other kids. They like you, but you don't know why. Everyone around you acts like you fit in, so you try to fit in.

You grow older, and still, you just don't quite fit. You don't feel connected to other people. But you play along. You're in high school and you really can't let anyone know you feel this way. You never feel comfortable. Some days your skin crawls. You're nervous. You feel moments of panic like you are gasping for air. But no one knows because you're still blending. You look around and wonder what the secret is. Why are you never quite good enough? Meanwhile, you try to act normal and be the person people think you are.

But you're not who people think you are. Inside, you are a shaking, frightened teenager. It feels like you are under water—that little bit of panic right before your head surfaces. You feel different, and not in a good way. You can feel the pressure on your skin. And you have to get out. Because you're suffocating and no one has a clue.

Then one day, you're hanging out with friends and someone has something to drink or a drug. So you give it a try. Immediately you can feel your body coming up out of the water and you take a huge breath of air. You can feel the rush of relief. You can feel the warm sun on your face. You want to stretch your arms out and scream because you're not dead after all. For the first time in your life you can breathe, and it is fucking amazing after an entire life of suffocating. You are not just you—you are more you than you've ever been. You don't feel high—you feel like everyone else. Your skin stops crawling. You're not in complete panic. You are for the first time in your life alive and safe and calm. And you never want to go back to the way you were.

People who are not addicts do not have this reaction to drugs or alcohol. Normal people have a few drinks and feel a little floaty and think, That was fun. Or they take a pill for an injury or an illness, and feel kind of happy and silly. But the brain chemistry of an addict or alcoholic is completely different. A drug or a drink is a life changer. It's an awakening from a life spent in loneliness and fear. You have saved your own life. And once you're awake, your brain will never let you forget it. From that moment on your brain says, "Get it, get it, get it, get more, get more," and it never quiets. It is relentless. It is bigger than you. It's so loud it's deafening. To tell an addict or alcoholic to stop is the equivalent to saying, "Go back under the water." But that's impossible. An addict will do the most horrifying, demoralizing, immoral acts to avoid going back under the water where they will no doubt die.

So what do you do? You have to learn to live above the water without the drugs and booze—to feel the sun, and stretch your arms out and embrace and love life. You don't have to go back under the water, but you must find that tiny flame that burns in each of us and help it grow until that fire is so big, the stalking "get more" voice in your head shuts the fuck up. Until then, you must protect that tiny flame because at the end of the day, it will be the only thing to build a new life on.

The fact is that I am still struggling. I had six years in sobriety. Then one day I didn't anymore. But some day I will take that big breath of air without the aid of alcohol or drugs. I will choose life. One day I will be under the water, and the next I will be looking for something to pull me out. I won't self destruct to such a level that the flame inside me blows out. I can still feel the little flame in my heart, but right now it's like I've got my back to the wind and I'm cupping that flame with my hands.

Alcoholism and addiction is a lifetime deal. If I'm lucky (and most of us aren't), I will be around long enough to come out of the water without help and feed my fire. And then, I will feel peace.

There are five people in my family. My mom reads. My dad plays golf. He loves golf. My sister Jennifer is sixteen. My other sister April stays outside really late. I like to go to the water park with my family. I have two fish. Plumpie and Goldie. Kiwi is my favorite food. Corduroy is my favorite book. Grease is my favorite movie. Gymnastics is my favorite sport. My favorite game is Jenga. I collect baby feathers. I like to blow them up in the air.

Carly

six years old

High On Life

Carly had been to detox and she was doing well. She came and sat on my bed. She was so pretty. Seventeen years old. I don't know why, but the words just came out of my mouth and I wasn't even thinking about saying them: "Let me see your arms."

I must have caught her completely off guard because she just gave me a blank look and showed me her arms. I took one look, and a sickening thud hit the bottom of my stomach.

I turned away and pulled the blanket to my chin and closed my eyes. Carly sat silent.

After a few minutes, she said, "They're infected. I think I have to go to the emergency room." Andy, who had also relapsed, took Carly to the hospital.

I was lying on my bed with my eyes closed. I felt like I had to be completely still. My skin felt thin like if I took too deep a breath, I would rip apart.

It occurred to me that it was never going to end. The boyfriends would always be addicts. I didn't see Carly dating a sweet fellow who worked at the bank around the corner. I'd like that, but I didn't see it happening.

I also realized that I didn't know Carly anymore, and that I was going to watch her kill herself. Oh, God, help me. I can't do this anymore.

I thought over and over about what I was going to do when Carly overdosed and died. How would we go on? And then I knew: I wouldn't go on. And then I realized that it was just going to be too painful to actually have to watch her die. Right in front of me. My daughter was dying. That's when I snapped.

John is speeding down the freeway, taking me to the mental hospital. He is driving as if I have an enormous open wound that is bleeding all over the seats.

He has to drive that way because he is feeling the same things I am feeling. He knows. He is in the same pain and it frightens him. So he has to get me there fast before he snaps, too. We have spent the last four years of our lives suffocating with fear.

As we drive to the hospital, John is swerving in and out of traffic on the highway, crying and screaming, "These fucking kids are going to kill us!" I sit in the passenger seat, also crying. Two people swerving in and out of traffic with their hearts broken wide open.

I have to be clear. It wasn't Carly who sent me into the psychiatric ward, but she was the straw that broke the camel's back. Say I'm a camel, and I'm carrying forty-six years of complete chaos on my back. Eventually, it gets too heavy. Even for a big strong camel like me.

I thought it was the end of the road. I told John I just couldn't do it anymore. I can't say I wanted to die. I just didn't really want to live anymore. I just didn't want to feel the pain. And if that meant not being here anymore, fine. I was tired of being sad, and tired of being tired.

But it wasn't the end. It turned out to be the beginning.

At the hospital, they take my belt and my shoelaces. They take the clip in my hair.

I say, "Why can't I have a clip in my hair?"

They say it could be used as an instrument to kill myself.

How many times would I have to stab myself with a hair clip to actually achieve death? Five hundred times? Six hundred times? That would take all day. I give them the hair clip.

An orderly and John escort me through about a zillion locked doors to my "unit." John kisses me and tells me everything will be okay, and then he is buzzed out.

I walk into my unit and an older man says, "You got a nice body. I'm not taking my water pills, so I'm not pissing my pants anymore."

I think, Finally...my people.

My room at the hospital is okay except they keep the air conditioning at around sixty degrees. My roommate is adorable. She has suffered from depression all her life, but she is still good for a laugh.

She is getting shock treatments, and every other day I have to reintroduce myself because her memory is gone for a few days after each treatment. Her memory starts to come back, but then she gets another treatment. It's like the movie "Groundhog Day."

I say, "Hi, I'm Dina, your roommate. You told me yesterday to remind you that you owe me twenty bucks."

She smiles sweetly and lies down for hours.

There were all kinds of people at the hospital. One guy was in the Broadway play *Rent*. Another guy could sit down and play the piano like he was doing a concert. Another guy was an artist. A lot of very talented broken people.

The water pill man was kicked off another unit, so he had to have a "tech" follow him everywhere he went. He sang from the top of his lungs, and then did karate-like moves with no warning. He was about sixty, but he picked fights with the young buff patients on the unit.

He said, "Are you looking at me? Because I'm ready when you are."

They laughed and said, "I'm not ready yet."

And he said, "I didn't think you were. You're nothing but a girl."

They had group therapy four or five times a day. In each group, they asked how you were feeling, and then they wrote it down. So they asked me how I was feeling, and I said, "I'm high on life." Then they scribbled in their notebooks.

The pill window was the most popular place to be. On the mental ward, they did anything to keep people from flipping out. So you lined up at the "med" window, and they gave you whatever your doctor said you were allowed to have. I wasn't allowed very many things. Some people got really great drugs. I was robbed.

Some people were at the pill window every half hour or so. The nurse would tell them they couldn't have their pills for another hour, and they would say they had heard voices and the voices said it was time for pills. Other people took so many pills that they were falling asleep and couldn't understand anything.

The pills they gave the water pill guy were supposed to calm him down and give us a break from his bullshit, but they only made him sing louder—and then one day, he started trying to throw things over the wall to the unit that kicked him out. I mean he was throwing chairs and garbage cans. He hurled a giant metal chair over the wall and screamed, "How do you like that, bitches?"

No one on the unit could stand this old man, but for me he was a constant source of entertainment. I realize that it's probably not right to see humor in a crazy person. But I think he would appreciate me seeing him as entertaining rather than seeing him as crazy. I tried to talk to him one day. He told me he had been in and out of institutions and jails since he was fourteen. He said there was nothing he couldn't do, and as soon as he got out, he was going to start a Walk for Peace program—and also file a grievance against the hospital because they were bullshit motherfuckers.

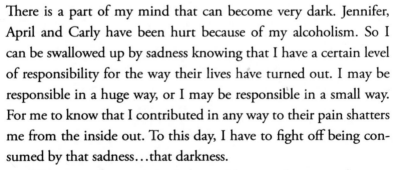

There is a part of my mind that can become very dark. Jennifer, April and Carly have been hurt because of my alcoholism. So I can be swallowed up by sadness knowing that I have a certain level of responsibility for the way their lives have turned out. I may be responsible in a huge way, or I may be responsible in a small way. For me to know that I contributed in any way to their pain shatters me from the inside out. To this day, I have to fight off being consumed by that sadness...that darkness.

My reason for not wanting to stick around was not because of Carly's drug addiction. It was because I felt she wouldn't have become an addict in the first place if I had made better choices. When you've done the wrong thing by your children, that's a giant pill to swallow every day. Nothing else in life matters as much. How much money you make, your great job, your pretty clothes—none of it means anything. If you fail your children, you have failed.

———— ∞ ————

I was in the hospital for eight days, which is a very short stay by "going mental" standards.

My doctor said it was exhaustion and that I needed to find a way to get more rest and less stress.

On my way out, the water pill man said, "Here's my number. Call me if you need anything, ever, and I'll take care of it because I have contacts everywhere, even overseas."

I said thank you and hugged him.

Then I left, and as soon as I got in the car, I put on my belt, I put on my shoelaces, and I put my clip back in my hair.

High on life.

I think of all those people in the hospital, and I realize I gained a little piece of warmth and hope from my stay, which is something I didn't go in with. I pray they will all be well and happy and find a way to work through it. I feel good. I think for me it was a one-time overwhelming feeling that put me there, and that I won't be back.

After years of tormenting myself, what I've decided is that I have to forgive myself, which is something that doesn't come overnight. I have to work at it every day. I've also realized that it will drive me crazy trying to help the girls and be a wife and grandmother. No good can come from trying to do it all. Which is why I ended up in the mental ward.

———— ∞ ————

One time when I visited Carly in rehab, she said she was thinking about becoming an attorney. I told her she would be a great one. I told her at first she would have to be a public defender and defend people who don't have a lawyer. I also told her that often lawyers have to defend people they know are guilty, but they have a right to be defended.

I told her, "For example, you are given a case for a guy who ran into his mother's trailer with his car, drunk, after a violent fight, and knocked her trailer over, killing her. But you have to defend him and convince a judge or jury that he is somehow innocent."

Without even a pause, Carly said, "It wasn't his fault that the trailer fell over because it wasn't secured to the foundation."

I wish she'd use her power for good instead of evil.

Carly may continue to relapse. April may drink forever. Jen may flow in and out of sobriety. There is nothing I can do about their addictions and choices. I can only navigate my own demons and go to sleep at night with the choices I've made that day. And some days, it isn't pretty.

I can help with Moses. I can take care of Mom. I can work and do the best I can to keep John thrilled to be in my presence. That's it. Life has to go on.

Carly is nineteen. When you turn eighteen, other treatment options open up. People under eighteen are simply screwed. Each state has a certain number of dollars for drug treatment. Almost none of it goes to adolescents—and the money that is approved for them is mostly for outpatient treatment like counseling.

Our country is stuck in the 1980s, when teenagers were sneaking behind the bleachers at football games, drinking cheap beer and smoking pot. No one wants to know that we have four-teen- and fifteen-year-old intravenous heroin addicts. Crystal meth is completely taking over our communities. Drug dealers are now dealing more prescription medications than illegal drugs. These prescription drugs are resulting in fifteen-year-olds over-dosing and dying all across our country. All of this sounds very dramatic. I wish I was just being dramatic. I'm being truthful. Teenage addicts have no place to go unless they come from some sort of money or their families have access to money. A large pile of money. They have no options. They are treated like they are just misbehaving or acting out, when in reality, they are hard-core addicts.

Our society—we—set them on a certain path. From what I can see, there are two ways to go. We can set them on a path of treatment, recovery, faith, hope, and a future. But that would require drug and alcohol treatment, and that, of course, requires money. The second path—and the one we are currently utiliz-ing—is putting them in youth jails. Detention centers. This sets them on another path, which consists of a life in and out of these kinds of places. There are young people who come out of deten-tion centers and never use again because they don't want to go back. But that's rare. Usually they end up being in and out of jails for many years.

And what does this cost? What does it cost in terms of the crimes they are committing? What about the cost of their medical problems? What about the cost of law enforcement and courts? What about the cost to the community? What does it cost to have these people sit in jail?

I dropped out of high school in the ninth grade, so I am not a math genius. But wouldn't it be cheaper to provide these kids with medical treatment? The War on Drugs is actually a war on people. Especially on our young people. But I think most people don't want to acknowledge the seriousness of the drug problem, let alone acknowledge that we're approaching it the wrong way. People just don't want to believe this is really happening. Or they say, "Not my kid." Thank God it's not your kid. But that's what I said, too. I was wrong. Today, it's my kids. Tomorrow, it could be yours.

I am not a fan of a revolving rehab door. I feel that jail can be used as a tool after an addict has been through treatment, has had a spiritual experience with a higher power, and dug deep within themselves to find where the pain is coming from. Then, to end up in jail and have that time to allow those things to surface could assist in their recovery. But it should be the last resort. Not the first.

Carly and Andy moved into their own apartment. I had a feeling something was wrong because we hadn't heard from them in a while, and when we went to the apartment, they didn't answer the door.

Then on Mother's Day, I got a phone call from Carly.

Carly: "Hurry and come pick me up. Hurry." Then she hangs up.

I get to the apartment, walk around the corner to their building, and I see Andy sitting in the dirt, covered with blood and crying. There are people from other apartments standing on their balconies looking down at him.

I run to him and say, "My God! What happened?"

He stands up, still crying, and says, "Happy Mother's Day." And walks away.

I think, Holy shit, and run up to the apartment. Carly is

standing there, intact, no blood, but the entire apartment is destroyed. Every single thing is broken. There is glass everywhere. All the furniture tipped over, broken, like nothing I've ever seen before.

I put Carly and her dog in the car and take them to my house. On the way, she explains that she and Andy have been using meth to get off heroin. Andy thinks that Carly is a police officer and she is setting him up, so he destroyed the apartment. He actually thought the dog had a recording device planted under its skin somewhere.

We get home and no more than four hours later, Andy calls. Carly talks to him and then hangs up the phone and says she has to go back with Andy.

I know enough to know this means that she's beginning to withdraw, therefore she has to get back to the apartment.

Carly says Andy is really sorry and she loves him and they are going to get clean together.

Andy comes to pick her up, and because Carly is now legally an adult, there's nothing John or I can do. Of course, we scream at her the entire time it takes Andy to come to pick her up, and then we scream at him. Then we watch them drive away.

Over the next week, I convince both of them to go into separate rehabs. I make arrangements for Carly, and Andy's family makes arrangements for him. We move them out of the apartment, and they both go into treatment.

The decision-making part of the brain of an individual who has been using crystal meth is very interesting. When Carly and Andy were in their apartment, they ran out of drugs. They sold every single thing they had except two things: a couch and a blow torch.

They had to make a decision because something had to be sold to buy more drugs. A normal person would automatically think, Sell the blow torch. But Andy and Carly sat on the couch, looking at the couch and looking at the blow torch, and the choice brought intense confusion. The couch? The blow torch? I mean, we may not need the blow torch today, but what about tomorrow? If we sell the couch, we can still sit wherever we want. If we move some of this glass, we could sit on the floor, or on the kitchen counter, or on the window ledge. But the blow torch? A blow torch is a very specific item. If you're doing a project and you need a blow torch, you can't substitute something else for it. You would have to have a blow torch, right?

In the end, they sold the couch. So when we moved them out, that was it: a blow torch. Although moving someone when all they have is a blow torch makes for an easy move.

Carly went into a three-month drug treatment facility in another city. Andy went into a treatment center in town.

We went to see Andy in treatment. He was, as they say, "thriving" in rehab. He really needed a job when he got out, but he had sold his car, so he didn't even have a way to get to work. So John and I made a deal: John would give Andy a job and they would work together. And since Carly was gone, Andy could stay with us as long as he completed his rehab and then went to outpatient treatment for two months.

The frustrating part is that even when an addict or alcoholic goes into treatment, that doesn't mean they are "cured." Most relapse. Most relapse over and over. Most people need to be in a drug treatment as many times as it takes. The encouraging part about this is that while they are in treatment, learning something, hoping to evolve into a spiritual human being, they are not carjacking you on your way home from work.

A few weeks later, Carly finally came home, too. We were so excited. It was like a holiday. And she was happy to be home.

She walked in the house and hugged and kissed her dog, and then went into her room and got on her bed and screamed, "My bed!" Andy was with her and he had also been clean for three months. Andy and Carly were both clean and happy.

She came home on a Wednesday. By Friday morning, we had a problem.

I am unloading the dishwasher in the kitchen when Carly walks in. I look at her and see that she is grinding her teeth.

I look back down at the dishes and think, No, not really. It just can't be. I look back up and sure enough, she is high.

We fight back and forth for about an hour, with me screaming the "fuck" word every three seconds. Then her crying, then me crying.

An hour later, she admits she is high. So is Andy.

I say, "Get out."

John walks in not knowing what's going on. I tell him they are both high and both leaving. Then John starts screaming. Then Jen walks in and starts screaming. Then Carly and Andy pack a bag and leave, walking.

I call the rehab Carly had just left. They say they can take her back if she comes back in the next couple of days before they close her paperwork.

I call Carly and say, "You can come home when you're

ready to go back to rehab. But they're not going to just hold a bed especially for you until you're ready. You're not going to get high for weeks, and then expect they will take you back."

Carly says, "I don't want to go back. I want to go to a half-way house."

So I say, "I'll pick you up and we'll find a halfway house."

Carly says, "I won't go without Andy."

"Well then, sit there with Andy. Call me when you want to get clean." I hang up.

Days later Carly called. She was high and hysterical. Andy was hysterical. I told her I needed to know where they were. She said she didn't know. Hours later we found them in a crack apartment. If you took a map and pinpointed the asshole of Phoenix, it would be where the apartment was located. I took both of them to the emergency room hoping the hospital would relocate them to a detox. The doctor checked them over and released them. No detox.

At that point, Carly had been home for a week, and she had been high on meth and heroin for four days. I called Andy's father and said Carly and Andy were going to be released from the hospital, and that Andy was about to become a homeless person. Andy's dad said he would come pick Andy up. I took Carly home. She continued to argue with me about going back into rehab. We argued and argued.

The next day I was exhausted. I lay down on my bed and said a prayer. I told God I didn't know what to do. I didn't have any more strength or answers.

Ten seconds later, I jumped off the bed, went to Carly's room and said, "You have half an hour to shower and pack your bag."

I pointed at the bag that was still packed from when she came home. "If you don't pack your bag with the things you want, we will take what you have in there right now. Get up. You have half an hour."

I dialed the number to the rehab and handed the phone to Carly. "Tell them you're coming back," I said.

She said, "This is bullshit. You can't force me."

I said, "Dad is in the other room. He'll pick you up like a rag doll and throw you in the car. Tell them you're on your way back and make it fast because now you only have twenty minutes."

Twenty minutes later, John and Carly and I were walking out the door. Carly was suddenly in a better mood. She hugged her dog and said, "I'm sorry, Squirty. I just need more time. I love you."

So John and I drove Carly back to Tucson. And on the two-and-a-half hour trip, her attitude became better. She talked about how it was possible that she needed more time in rehab. She was also thankful that they were willing to take her back.

We brought in all her things, and they welcomed her back. John and I again drove away, exhausted, but relieved.

After Carly was gone, Andy came by to apologize. We appreciated it, but told him they seem to fuel each other's drug addictions. I think Carly and Andy are also starting to realize this. Now the question is, if you love someone but are not good for each other, do you stay away or do you die together?

Carly came home after three months away, and this time it seemed like she was really getting the idea of how to stay clean. Andy was also clean. And Carly and Andy were still inseparable. I couldn't have asked for anything more. They were both clean.

Finally.

I jokingly said to Carly that I needed a big finish for my book. I needed the house to burn down, or the car to explode just as I was walking away from it. Something big.

Right then Carly hurled a Tootsie Roll at me at about three hundred miles an hour. It hit me in the hand. I thought my hand was shattered.

Carly said, "You needed a big ending." Then she rolled on the floor laughing.

That's my big ending? I get hit by a Tootsie Roll? Do you read books? Not one person will read this book and say, "It's the book about how a lady got hit by a Tootsie Roll." Even if she shattered my hand and my whole arm, it still isn't enough. Now if she had hit me in the throat and the Tootsie Roll lodged itself in my windpipe, that's an ending. Fucking kids.

Seven months after rehab, Carly was still clean. She had a job. She quit smoking. She ran every day. She ate carrots and granola. It was confusing. I thought, Can I let go of the fear? Are the girls growing up a little bit? Growing up enough to know that all the trauma isn't worth the price they have to pay the following day? It was quiet. Knock wood. Burn some candles. Roast a pig.

Carly had three ideas for a big ending for my book other than hitting me with candy. She said she and Andy could get married. They could have a baby. Or they could relapse. All bad ideas.

I was feeling really good about life. The girls were doing well. The sun was shining. I was thankful for everything.

I thought, Yes, I can let go of fearing everything is going to crash to the ground at any second. What if we became a completely normal family? That would be insane. I loved the idea. Yes. Let go of the fear.

Then I walked into Carly's room. She was holding her dinner plate full of food, hugging it sitting up, asleep, with food all over her lap.

So, okay, she was high on heroin. There is no better way to say it other than it boggles the fucking mind.

I thought she was clean. But Carly and Andy had been using heroin for the last three months, and we didn't have a clue. Looking back, I could see it. But when I was in it, I couldn't see it. It's like it was so close to my face that I simply didn't see it happening.

Opiates aren't as easy to recognize as you would think. As long as a person "maintains" and doesn't overdo it (at least until their parents go to sleep), you could pretend to be normal for a while. But eventually you will overdo it and end up hugging a plate with chicken all over your lap.

Methamphetamines, on the other hand, I can spot a hundred miles away. People on meth are usually taking things apart and putting them back together.

Andy took a washing machine completely apart to find the recording device the FBI put in there to bust him with drugs. He also did this with cell phones and televisions. I love you, Andy, but the FBI has bigger fish to fry. But you can't explain that to someone who hasn't slept or eaten for nine days.

So I tried to find Carly a detox. I went to the usual places, but found out they no longer accepted state-funded insurance. They told me there was only one place, with two locations, to go to detox in the entire city of Phoenix. One location was full, but the hospital was able to get Carly into the other. It was in downtown Phoenix, and she would have to go by ambulance.

The ambulance drivers took Carly and they rolled her into detox hell. They said later they didn't feel like it was safe for them to drop her off there. But the lady at the desk explained that this was the only place in the city to leave her. So they left her.

These two different locations obviously couldn't handle all of the detoxing drug addicts in a city the size of Phoenix. So they had a process to weed out the sick people. They put them on a bed in a room with a bunch of other beds. They give them a bed pan to vomit in, and tell them if they want to leave, to sign out and leave. So as the addict becomes increasingly ill, she knows she can leave and use at any point. They say they only help the ones who fight off the withdrawal because this shows who really wants help. Many of the sick people walk out.

I know people might say, "Fuck them...if they really want to get clean, they will stay." I say fuck the process that makes people prove they would rather have seizures and vomit repeatedly and have cramps from their heads to their toes, than leave and walk down one block and feel better in seconds. A person says they want to change their life and this is how we help them?

In defense of the facility, how the hell are they supposed to treat an entire city of people nobody wants? What would happen if all these fucked-up, high people sat on the steps of the White House and said, "We aren't leaving until we get medical treatment"?

The people on crystal meth would say, "Let's tear this bitch down then rebuild it." The people on heroin would say, "Don't tear it down, man. I want to take a nap in the Red Room."

We continue to put sick people in prison when what they need is medical treatment. If you have to continuously build bigger prisons, isn't that a clear indication that the plan isn't working? Because if it was working, and people were "learning a lesson" by being locked up, wouldn't the prison population become smaller?

As it turned out, Carly "passed" the test. She didn't leave, and she eventually went back into the rehab she had previously been in.

Since Carly turned eighteen, she has been able to get treatment at a state-funded rehab center. Before that, the only way to get help for her was through our health insurance, which involved thousands of phone calls and lots of screaming and begging for help.

Always remember, "no" doesn't mean "no" with insurance companies. If you think your kid is going to die, do not accept "no." Stalk the insurance company until they get so tired of you they agree to pay for treatment. When you're talking to someone, ask to talk to their boss, and then to their boss, and so on until they hear your crazy voice on the phone and they crack. Ask them what they would do if it was their child. Tell them about your child, and tell them how much you love your child. I've learned to balance anger with kindness. Utilize the saying, "You catch more bees with honey than you do with vinegar." In the end, your kid will probably get treatment. "No" doesn't mean "no." But speak from your heart, because the person on the other end of the phone also has a heart. You hope.

It had been about a week since Carly's latest trip to rehab, and John and I were feeling sort of low. The therapists at the rehab told us we should "nurture" our marriage. Of course, that means something different to John than it does to me. As far as I'm concerned, the best place for "nurturing" is Vegas, so off we went with our sad little hearts.

We arrive in Vegas and check into our room. John lies down, and I go into the bathroom and start a bath.

I come back around the corner and see John lying on the bed, clutching his chest and dripping with sweat. I mean, soaking wet. Buckets of sweat are running down his face. He says he feels like he is being crushed.

I call 911 and describe John's symptoms. They say he is having a heart attack. That sounds so bizarre that I say, "When you say 'heart attack,' you mean, he's having a heart attack and he just needs some rest and tomorrow he'll be okay? Right?" They send an ambulance to take John to the hospital.

At the hospital, a doctor says John is having a massive heart attack, but they can't handle a heart attack of this level at this hospital. So they put John back in the ambulance and take him to another hospital. I ride in the ambulance with John, and then follow as they push John's gurney through the hallways, and then into an operating room where doctors are waiting, dressed to fix him. They tell me I can't go in, and the double doors shut in front of me. I stand there, alone, staring at the doors.

The only place we have ever gone in Vegas is casinos. The hospital is beautiful, and I can't help but think, They didn't build this place on "winners."

───── ⣿ ─────

I was terrified. My sister flew in that night. John's sister, Cheryl, and our niece, Michelle, drove in, so that made my panic subside. John's son, Michael, was in Vegas, so he came to the hospital, too. I felt better surrounded by familiar faces.

John had two blocked arteries. One they unblocked, and the other they said they couldn't fix because it wasn't safe. I guess it's located under and around the back of his heart. On the one they fixed, they used a thing called a "stent." It goes into the artery and blows it open with a balloon.

To hear the doctors talk, they do this procedure thousands of times a day. Like I guess most people have a stent, which means most people in the world have had a tube shoved up their groin, all in the effort to blow open the artery in their heart. The doctors make it sound simple. You could be standing in line at Starbucks, and you could have your artery blown open by the time they prepare your Grande Carmel Macchiato. They make it sound like maybe I should get a stent as well, because everybody who's anybody has a stent. Seriously. Google it.

John was lying in the intensive care unit, bleeding out of his groin area, so we had to wait for days until it stopped. Lisa, Cheryl, and Michelle left. So it was just me and Michael sitting in the room.

I didn't know how I would cope without John. One minute, we were a team together. Five minutes later, I could be alone. I remember being so filled with fear. So afraid I couldn't speak. I remember watching the door to the operating room shut in front of me, and just standing there, completely silent, trying to comprehend what was happening and wondering what would happen to my head if they came out of those doors and told me something I couldn't hear.

Later, I was sitting alone in a corner of the waiting room, staring at a fish tank. I was thinking, John is my guy, and my biggest fear is that the world would be empty without him. John tells me I'm pretty. John makes me laugh. John has always been the one who loves us.

John was in intensive care for seven days, and then they said he could go home. They say what happens in Vegas stays in Vegas. Not always. It's like one minute you're sitting at a slot machine waiting for three Wayne Newton heads to come up, and the next minute, you're having a stent shoved up your privates. Life is trippy.

We got home from the heart attack trip, and I felt over-whelmed with responsibility. I was already overwhelmed, but I was able to handle it because John was my helper. Now, I had no helper and another really sick person to care for.

At work, it felt like a bolt had been twisted in my brain because now I was even more stuck there. We needed our health insurance more than ever because a massive heart attack is expensive. John's medi-cations alone would have been twelve hundred dollars a month if we didn't have health insurance. So the weight of work, with the huddles, and signing this and that, and your smile is part of your uniform, and the people are your flesh and blood, all of it—it felt like a crushing weight. It felt like, "You can't do one wrong thing or you'll get fired and your life will be destroyed and John will have a heart attack and die and it will be your fault." Holy fucking shit!

The doctor told me not to allow John to have stress. What? Every single thing in our lives involves the word "stress." The girls, Mom, financial problems. So anything that happened, I had to hide it from John and deal with it and make sure no one upset him.

At that point, the twin had been living with us for six months. Having him there was daily stress, and it got worse after John's heart attack. I was suffocating, and every time I looked at Geo, I wanted to unleash on him with an ice pick. I mean, I didn't do that, but I really, really wanted to. I really wanted this. I would just surprise him. With an ice pick. It was nice to imagine.

"How heavy are the weights?" I ask, but then before he can answer, I scream, "I don't care! I don't care! I don't care!" Each time, over and over, with the ice pick. Again and again and again until I begin to sweat and fall exhausted to the floor. Then one more time for good measure. Then a few more times. Then one, two, three, four, five more times. Then one more time, but it doesn't even pierce his skin because I am so tired from all the stabbing, over and over and over. I drop the ice pick on the floor with compete satisfaction. Then, finally, silence.

I forgot my original point.

Oh, yeah. So I'd drive home from work, crying half the time because I hated my job so much. Then I'd walk in the front door to Geo, and he'd tell me a story about himself and how heavy his weights are and how far he ran, and the whole time I was wishing the roof would cave in and kill both of us. Meanwhile, Mom would be ringing her bell, and the dog would be staring at me, and everyone was starving, but John couldn't eat anything but wheat sticks.

I would take all the incoming problems and do the best I could. I'd situate the people in the house, and then go in the back room and close the door. I sat in the back room watching TV for months.

———— ∞∞ ————

After John got a little better, he went to Tucson with me so I could do a comedy job. I woke up that morning with a headache, John and I went to visit Carly in rehab, and then we drove to Tucson so I could do two shows that night.

When we go to Tucson we are fortunate to be able to stay in our dear friends' guest house way up in the hills. It's beautiful and peaceful and I would like to never leave. John and I have known these people for twenty years.

Okay, so the wife, Denise. Denise is as gorgeous as she was twenty years ago. I know people always say that, but in her case, it's actually true. She drinks a lot of wine, so we're thinking she's actually pickled. I on the other hand I have aged like a normal human.

Denise is one of those women who doesn't really know how beautiful she is, so that makes her more beautiful.

So that should be enough, don't you think? Beauty? Who needs more? Denise cooks all our meals when we stay with them. I don't mean grilled cheese. I mean Chicken a la Red Wine Marsala with Basil and Tomatoes—tomatoes that she hand-picked from some hill in Spain. Then she makes the salad dressing: Tomato a la Burberry Something Something. She prepares a different dish each evening.

I asked her, "What can I help with?"

She said, "Nothing. This dish is so simple. You relax."

Okay. So she's beautiful and she can cook. She and her husband also own a comedy club. We walked through the doors of the club, and I noticed since my last visit there was beautiful artwork covering the walls.

I said, "Wow. This looks amazing!"

Denise then proceeded to explain how she painted each piece of art, and how painting isn't really her thing but they needed something on the walls, so a girl does what she has to do.

What?

We went back to their home in the hills, and I demanded that I be allowed to do the dishes, without question. I was washing and I saw this wildly fantastic ceramic bowl. I was carefully washing it, thinking it was probably expensive and I didn't want to break it. I carefully turned it over and on the bottom of the dish it said, "by Denise B." At this point, I hung my head and turned to her and moaned, "You make your own dishes?"

The point I'm making is, could God spread it around a little? Why heap all the beauty and talent on a few people? If someone is short, make them really funny. If someone is bald, give them lots of money. On the other hand, if someone is beautiful, give them a constant toothache. Or if a person is a gifted artist, maybe they could have herpes.

It seems like God is in the people-making factory, and Jennifer Aniston comes down the belt and he takes his bucket of beauty and talent and dumps a shitload on her. Then Danny DeVito rolls by and God walks away to check his Facebook.

Back at Denise's, I set my drink on a table. Then I picked it back up and asked for a coaster because I don't want to ruin the beautiful table.

Denise said, "Oh, please. That table is so old. I made it when we lived in Germany."

I laughed and said, "Of course you did. We all made a table or two. In Germany."

God could spread the sweet sauce a little more evenly.

So that particular Friday, I was done with my two shows, and we were back at the house. But as that day progressed, my headache had become a migraine.

We were sitting outside by Denise's waterfall, on chairs that Denise welded together with scrap metal from an old washing machine. The seat cushions were covered with skin from a zebra that she harpooned while she was on a trip to South Africa.

For a fleeting second, I felt sad that a zebra had to die to make these beautiful cushions. But, man, zebra skin is so soft to sit on.

A week before our trip, John had a kidney stone (as if he hadn't been physically tortured enough). So I knew he had painkillers. I wasn't in my painkiller stage anymore, but my head felt like it was going to explode. So I said to John, "Give me half of one of your painkillers."

That was the beginning of a beautiful life. We woke up the next morning, and Denise was making crepes. We ate, hugged Denise and her husband goodbye, and then went back to Phoenix where we had a freezer filled with Swanson frozen entrées. Over the next week, I took all of John's painkillers.

I call the doctor and say, "John needs more." They call it in, and I show up at the pharmacy. Smiling. They go into "Don't drive or operate things." I'm thinking, Divine Order.

I take all of those. So now I have to go to the emergency room for fictitious pain. I have to act the whole thing out. I hurt my back. I think my knee is broken. I hurt my feelings. Whatever.

One time I say it is a toothache. Then the doctor walks in, and I say, "I was lifting my mother and I hurt my back."

He looks at his chart. "It says you have a toothache."

I say, "That too."

Then I make a huge mistake (aside from taking the painkillers in the first place): I begin to take them at work. I take a large painkiller when I am almost at work. I walk in and I have never been so happy to be a part of the team. I am beyond thrilled to be here.

I scan and scan, and all the foods are so interesting. The packaging is brilliant. The frozen Jolly Green Giant vegetables are such a striking color of green that I actually think I am in Ireland. The customers are like my own flesh and blood.

Random Man comes to my lane, and the anticipation of what information he is going to give me today makes me think I am going to explode with excitement!

Ballsack says, "I can really see an improvement in your attitude."

I say, "And I can see an improvement in yours! What color is that shirt? Eggplant? Love it! Eggplant is hot right now."

Then, as if it couldn't get any better, I take another large pill when I am almost home. I walk in the door, and thank God, Geo is standing there telling a long story about himself! I cannot wait to hear about the heavy weights! Or about the abnormal distances he is running. Everything he says about himself completely intrigues me! He is so interesting! And the tone of his voice doesn't sound like nails on a chalkboard anymore! It sounds like Celine Dion singing that Titanic song.

Everything is better. Everything.

It had to end. All of this happiness was simply getting out of control.

Every time I walked into the pharmacy, I said, "This is the last time." Carly was about to come home after six months in rehab. The last thing she needed was her mother jumping up and down on the furniture. So no more pills.

It sounds easy enough, right? Wrong. I had been taking Klonopin for two years. So I had to spend two days in the hospital to make sure I didn't have a seizure or a heart attack or a mental breakdown. I got out of the hospital, and I was sick for two weeks. But every day, I just carried on like I was fine, and each day I got a little better. The exact way I felt was expressed by an addict on TV. He said, "Nothing is making me happy right now." Exactly. But I felt "happier" every day that passed. Today, I am quickly approaching happy.

The pain pills gave me this insane energy. But then I stopped taking them, and I went back to feeling drained all the time. I said to Carly, who is a horrible influence on me, "What if I drank one of those energy drinks?" I had never had one. Carly drank them all day.

She completely encouraged me to try one, and I do not feel I had my own free will in this situation. I drank one, and the next thing I knew, I wanted to build a wooden deck on to the back of the house. I cleaned out my closet. I did all the laundry. I organized all the books on all three of my bookshelves in alphabetical order, like the library. All of these activities took half an hour. My sister, Lisa, said the energy drinks are not good for me. I said they are good for me and I like it and I'm not going to stop. Or sleep.

When the pain pill party ended, some things had to change. It had to happen. By this time Geo had been living with us for eight months. I asked Geo to move out. I went back to my job with the same depressed feelings. All my coworkers were twenty years old. I was forty-eight. From lifting things at work for ten years and lifting Mom for four years, every part of me hurt. Not I-need-a-painkiller hurt, but I-can't-physically-do-this-job-anymore hurt. Everything was pulled and twisted. The doctor said I had a torn meniscus in my knee. Who cares? I was falling apart. The Green Giant vegetable bag was not that fucking great. My job sucked. Period.

Things went from bad to really bad. I hated having to do these stupid degrading things at work. I hated being spoken to like I was stupid by bosses who were younger than my kids. I hated having to ask a twenty-year-old for permission to go to the bathroom. I was way too old for this shit, but I had to have the health insurance. So no matter what one of my bosses said, I had to suck it up.

It was clear to me that there would never be a convenient time to quit my job as a checker. I would scan groceries until I dropped dead. That was my reality. There would never be a day when John would come to me and say, "Quit that shitty job." I had waited ten years for some sort of approval to quit scanning groceries. It was not going to happen.

And our health insurance? And John's heart condition? John will have a heart condition for the rest of his life, so that is how long I would have to check groceries. I would have to check groceries for the next twenty years. I would have to stand on that mat for the next twenty years, smiling, for health insurance. Suck it up.

John's heart attack drove me to the conclusion that life could end at any moment. And I am working a job that is actually making me physically ill, and I have to do this for another twenty years?

I know most people hate their jobs. But ideally, I think a job should be a place where maybe you're not thrilled to be there, but some days are okay.

It should not be a place you hate so much your stomach is in knots all day.

It should not be a place where you have to stand on the black mat behind your register because you've been told not to step off of it or a twenty-two-year-old will snap his fingers and point for you to step back on the mat.

It should not be a place where you're constantly told to uncross your arms, smile bigger, and stand up straighter.

It should not be a place where you're not allowed to go to the bathroom during your period, even as the blood drips down your leg. I said, "I can't control this." I was told, "You better figure out a way to control it. Turn around and check groceries."

I was saying something to my boss one day, and as I was speaking he interrupted me and said, "You talk too much." And he walked away. But this wasn't unusual. Things like this are said to menial workers all the time. It's completely acceptable. There's a good chance I could remember at least one rude, shitty comment said by a boss for each day I worked there.

Nothing in particular happened that day. Nothing in particular was said. It was a day like any other. I clocked out and told my coworkers I'd see them tomorrow. I do not know what happened to my brain that day, but as I walked out the front door, the sun hit me in the face and in my head I thought, *I will never come back.* That was it. I had had enough. I worked there ten years. I was done. I didn't get fired. I didn't quit. I simply clocked out and never clocked back in. I never went back.

I guess they call it a leap of faith. It was my Oprah "light bulb" moment. I didn't have any fear or regret. I was solid and clear in my brain. I felt relaxed. I felt happy. I felt completely calm. I drove away and in the rearview mirror I looked at the store and said out loud, "See ya."

Let me defend myself. I had every job I have ever had in my life for at least five years. I am not a job quitter. I have worked my ass off at every job I have ever had. I know I need to work. I have a family. But I need to work someplace where I'm not climbing out of my skin every day. My adventure into pills was the result of feeling so backed into a corner…like I had no choices in my life…like I had to work this job…like I had to have my brother-in-law lying on my couch.

That does not excuse my behavior. People every day feel that same way and don't spend months taking painkillers. They also don't quit their jobs. My life didn't become unmanageable over-night. It was becoming unmanageable for a long time. I ignored it and turned my head away hoping it would get fixed by the time I turned around. The problems with my job and my brother-in-law existed for a long, long time. Years. But I didn't do anything to change it. I allowed myself to be consumed by it. I dropped out. I went in the back bedroom and shut the door, lay on the bed, took a pill or two, and stared at the TV. I did this for months. On the other side of the door was Geo, Mom, the girls, John with a heart condition, and my job. All alone in the back room it was just me, the TV, the remote, and the magic pills. I clocked out.

I didn't feel proud of myself when I stopped taking pills. I felt shame. I felt stupid. I felt I was a bad example. I felt I had let everyone down. I felt depressed. After those feelings sat in the pit of my stomach for a few weeks, I had to walk it off. The only thing to do was keep walking down the road, minus the happy pills. To go ahead and face the day with whatever came up and deal with it.

———— ⬥ ————

Change didn't come easy and it came with a price. But I have never wondered whether I did the right thing. It's like being in a really bad marriage. You know when you're walking down the aisle. When I went to work my very first day at the grocery store, I thought, Wow, this is going to suck. But I did what I had to do. I scanned and smiled for ten years.

Making choices and changes often brings explosions. But I am fortunate to have a husband who supported my decision, and when the flames died down, I didn't have a single regret. Shove my eighty percent PSS up your asses, douche bags.

I say to John and the girls, "I quit my job. I'm going to write a book. We're going to see some hard times, but I need you guys to support me on this."

I have been wearing my pajamas for almost a month, and we don't have any milk. I am for the first time in my life a starving artist, and I think I like it.

Hey, Dad. I get it.

I have put my parents through more painful shit than your whole family's painful shit all put together. They are so strong. God gave them three crazy fucking difficult-as-fuck-to-deal-with daughters. I'm sure he knew they were strong enough to handle it. But sometimes I think he's asking too much of them. I just want them to know I love them so fucking much. I want them not to hurt when they look at me. I want to be one of those girls who wouldn't ever even think about hanging out with me. One of those girls who is scared of needles and all the bullshit that comes with it. I just want to be me, the "me" God brought me here to be. Because it's for damn sure he didn't put me here to be a junkie.

Carly
seventeen years old.

A Letter From Dad

Carly,

I've been knee deep in some of the most pristine waters that one could imagine. I've seen snow come down so hard it blanketed an entire city. I've seen the Grand Canyon. I've seen skyscrapers that seem to reach to the heavens, and I've been atop mountains that have made me feel that I'm just a speck in the big picture.

None of those wondrous moments compare to the day God blessed me with the most beautiful daughter a father could have. I broke down and cried with joy. Never in my life did my heart feel so fulfilled as it was that day.

I had nothing to show for my struggles in my young life, but now I had a jewel named Carly.

That day I made a promise to myself with God as my witness that I would always be a part of this little girl's life. My life never got easier. But each and every day, I pushed forward in the hope that one day something special would happen in my life that would make my kids proud of me. That day has never come. I feel so empty and lifeless at times. Especially when I see other fathers provide so many things for their kids, like a home of their own, a special gift at graduation, a car, or even just a bedroom set they can call their own. My life consists of giving my kids an old used dresser that one of my family members deemed garbage, or clothes they no longer thought were in style, a TV set they were going to sell in a garage sale, or even a box spring and mattress that, of course, didn't come with a frame.

But as hard as life seems to be, I awake each morning to fulfill that promise I made on the day you were born. My wife needs me, my kids need me, and you know what? The world needs me. Because the one thing I can be proud of is that I have never left the side of the ones I cherish the most. I've fought and struggled for each and every thing I have in my life, but I have never ever had to fight or struggle to be a dad. My heart and soul are filled with so many wonderful memories, all because of my kids. I have the one thing in this world I would never trade for, and that's you...Carly, the jewel of my heart.

I write this to you because I feel the pain you have, I share the tears that run down your precious cheeks. You may be miles away from me, but I'm right there next to you as you read this letter. Feel me there, Carly. Feel the strength of a father's shoulder. Cry if you must. I hope it helps to know you will always have me to lean on.

Carly, if I could take your pain away, I would. But your pain is yours, and what you do with it will make you into the person you're going to be. Time heals, baby, I promise.

I assure you God only gives us what we can handle. You may think it's too much, but things will get better. A brighter day is right around the corner for you, but you have to go find it. Make your sunshine, baby. Make it shine for you.

My heart is with you my dear.
Dad

Every Story Has a Happy Ending If You Tell It Long Enough

Wouldn't it be great to have an ending where we are all saved and healthy and life is great? I love books that end like that. That's not how this book ends.

There are four stages of living with an alcoholic or drug addict:

Stage one: Confusion. When I got the phone call that Jennifer was using heroin, I was so confused and shocked I couldn't speak. She stopped, so I thought that was how it worked. Not so much. When Carly came to me and told me she was using OxyContin every day, I had no idea it was the beginning of what would be the most difficult years of our lives. That first stage lasts for a couple of years. The "this can't really be happening" stage.

The second stage is, "I will make you stop drinking and using drugs by showing you how much I love you!" This stage lasts until you end up in the mental hospital. I will fix the drug addict. I will never give up on the alcoholic. I will sacrifice my life for yours. Hello, mental ward.

The third and worst stage is, "You mean to tell me I really can't make her better with love?" This is the most crushing realization of all. It is a sad day when you really, deep in your heart, head, and spirit realize there is absolutely nothing you can do to keep them alive. It feels like you're drowning. You would do anything to make it stop. But it doesn't stop. In the end you're left exhausted and broken.

And then there is the fourth stage and the most important step you can take. It comes on the day you decide to live a life, or not. It comes on the day you realize, "I'm still here, breathing in and out." You can watch the kids walk into the fire, or you can go to the Olive Garden. You can cry because your heart is broken, or you can go to a movie. You can unravel because it's all unfair, or you can go to the beach. You can climb in the hole or climb out.

I don't think it's possible to avoid any of these stages because it's not based on simply making a decision. The ability to move on comes from within. It comes from knowing, but you can't know until your heart lets you.

I can remember the days, the years, and the events with the girls that brought all the walls in. John and I mentally caved in from the stress and heartbreak. There were years and years that we were barely able to lift our heads.

These days, the effects of all the years of tears and laughter have left John and me with an appreciation of the little things. Moses' smile. Squirt's enormous dog body. The color of my hair. Arguing about Jon and Kate.

My mom always says, "Tomorrow's another day." At least I think that's what she says. Although she may be saying, "There's a midget in my room shitting on my floor." Either way, I know what she's trying to say.

Every time I have to leave town to do a comedy job, my mom thinks I'm going to be on "American Idol." She says, "What song are you going to do?" Then I tell her that I'm doing standup comedy, not singing on "American Idol." She still doesn't get it and says, "Just don't do 'Somewhere Over the Rainbow.' That dark-haired girl will give you a run for your money." She's talking about Kelly Clarkson.

My mom and I used to talk and talk. She was the greatest person in the universe to have a laugh with. We would talk about everything and laugh until we cried.

But now, it's like she's not there anymore. Her eyes aren't even the same. I can't ask her a simple question because she doesn't understand—and if by chance she does respond, it's as if she's answering a completely different question. It's silence, then confusion.

Mom had never been on a vacation, ever. So we asked her, "If you could go anywhere, where would you go?"

She thought for a minute and then said, "Disneyland. I have never been to Disneyland." So we decided to take Mom to Disneyland.

We drive in two vehicles because we have to take Mom's toilet and her wheelchair. I shove them in the back of the Jeep, and it takes three people to push the door closed. Then we set out for Disneyland, the Happiest Place on Earth.

We make it to Los Angeles, but then we get lost for three hours. Every person in our caravan begins to melt down. I look out the window and notice the Burger King has bars on the windows.

We finally arrive at the hotel, exhausted, not one person speaking to another, except for the necessities: Someone bring in Grandma's toilet. Bed time. Go to hell. No, you go to hell.

After a good night's sleep, we all make up and drive across the street to the magic. It's time to go to Disneyland!

It seems like a thousand dollars later, but we are finally in. Mom is smiling. We are all smiling. This place is magic! It is almost 100 degrees, but that is okay. Everything is glittering and colorful.

I push Mom through the gate and say, "Here we go, Mom! We're at Disneyland!"

I get about ten feet when Mom's wheelchair very abruptly stops and lurches forward, almost hurling her out onto the golden brick road. I look down. Tracks. There are train tracks? I look ahead and realize there are train tracks everywhere. To get Mom's wheelchair over them, we all have to lift her so the wheels don't get wedged in the track. John and I look at each other and without saying a word, we know we have just entered hell.

Every few feet we lift, push for a few seconds, and then lift again. We are lifting the wheelchair with Mom in it when we hear the trolley making its way around the track. In the nick of time, we get Mom off the track, and the trolley passes with smiling people waving and having the time of their lives. John and I stare at them with sweat rolling down our faces.

The lines for the magic rides are about forty minutes. I understand why they sell three-day passes now. If you want to ride several of the rides, it will take three days.

By lunchtime, Moses' face is beet red. Mom is also getting sunburned. I slather both of them with sun block, just as I had done before we left. We are sitting in some sort of fairy restaurant after waiting for more than an hour. Moses refuses to eat. I tell him to eat his fairy burger. He has a screaming attack right in front of all the fairies. Then April begins to lose it, and then I begin to lose it, and we don't give a shit what the fairies are thinking. One hundred thirty-six dollars later, lunch is over. The fairies are not sorry to see us leave.

We go back out to the mean streets of Disneyland. The fun Disney characters are everywhere. Moses does not appreciate them one little bit. He cries every time one comes close to us. I try to wave them off, but they come anyway. Moses screams. I smile and tell the characters they are doing a great job.

The characters don't talk. They just do fun, silly body movements. I raise my hand to stop them, and they put their hands on their enormous bellies as if they are laughing and walk away in their giant outfits.

Mom wants to go on a ride, but the only ride in the magic kingdom that Mom can go on is "It's a Small World."

Because Mom is in a wheelchair—and because God had mercy on us—we don't have to wait in line. The entire family goes on the ride. We enter the tunnel, and immediately we are hit with the most beautiful cool air. We all realize our day just got better.

It turns out the world is not as small as you might have thought. The ride goes on forever, which is great. It is a fun ride with all the different countries and the music and air conditioning.

We come back out of the tunnel and pull up to the ride guy. We begin to stand and he says, "Wanna go again?"

We all look at each other, confused. Mom says, "Yes! We do!" So off we go, back into the air-conditioned tunnel.

Four times. We go through four times. That's how long it takes to lower our body temperatures to an almost normal level.

Afterwards, I am desperately looking for a tree to park

Mom under. I find one tree. There are about sixteen Japanese
people standing under it. They look like they are wedged into a
crowded elevator. Each of them has a camera hanging from his
neck. There is no way in.

We all have first degree burns. I stand in line for half an
hour to get water. Some to drink and some to dump on my family's heads to save their lives. Nineteen dollars later, I get the
water. Moses is bright red and crying in that miserable way
that children cry when they have really had enough—sobbing,
snot running out of his nose, rubbing his eyes. I am leaning
down, patting Moses' back, saying, "It's okay, Sweetie. I know,
I know…" when I see two enormous brown furry feet step into
our space. I look up. It is another giant cartoon character. He
waves. I say, "Please. Step away from the child."

The character does the same hand-on-the-belly laughing
thing as all the other characters and shuffles away.

I look at my family, and I can sense that the big people
could actually have some fun if they didn't have to worry about
lugging around a tired, sunburned baby and an old lady in a
wheelchair. I tell John to take us back to the room. And trust me,
it is no sacrifice on my part.

Mom and Moses and I get back into our room and it is
truly magic. We crank up the air, order room service, strip down
to our underwear, and climb in the big beautiful bed. We are
all thrilled. We eat cheeseburgers and chocolate shakes, and
watch TV. It is the best part of the trip. The three of us fall asleep
for about three hours with the nice air conditioning blowing on
our sunburned skin. Aaaah…life is great.

The others stay at Disneyland until late into the night, which
is great. They called several times saying, "Are you guys ready to

come back?"

I look at Moses sitting in his bath playing so peacefully, and Mom eating ice cream and watching something on TV. I say, "I don't think so. Really, we are fine."

Later in the evening, Moses and I take a walk and go swimming. It is nice and calm and fun.

I put Mom to bed in her little bedroom attached to our room. I am covering her and notice her window shade is open. Outside her window you can see Disneyland. Right at that moment, they begin a fireworks show.

I say, "Look, Mom. Fireworks!"

She watches as she lies in her bed. I call Moses in and he jumps up on the bed between me and Mom. Moses is pointing and smiling. Mom is smiling. There is complete silence...just beautiful, brilliant flashes of light and color filling the sky. The three of us lie there, hypnotized, each explosion greater than the last, and sometimes it feels like the fireworks are coming down on top of us. I look over at my mom. She looks happy. It seems like this is what she came for. The show goes on for about twenty minutes, and we watch all the way through.

When it is over, I close the shade, and pull the blanket over Mom's shoulders.

She says, "That was the best fireworks show I've ever seen."

I say, "Me too."

Right at that moment, I feel a connection to my mother that I have not felt in years. It is me and my mom watching the fireworks. It feels like we are both present for the first time in a long, long time. It is a moment I will never forget. It is magical.

I don't think moments are the things in life we plan. Like getting married or having children. Genuine moments happen when you aren't expecting them. Those are the things you remember all your life. Little snapshots that you can see as if they just happened. I went to bed grateful for that little bit of time with my mom, and I remembered just for a second what she used to be like.

We got home and it took six weeks to heal from the effects of Disneyland. We put the toilet back in Mom's bathroom and unloaded her wheelchair. I was happy Mom went to Disneyland, and she has an eighteen dollar coffee cup to prove she was there.

People always say, "You have to go to Disneyland. At least once." I agree. You have to go. At least once. But you know where the happiest place on earth is? My house. My bed. It turns out the best part of going to Disneyland is coming home.

I wanted my book to end like this: "Carly has been clean for seven years and now she's an astronaut. She will be the first heroin addict in space—and I mean real space. Jen and her longtime girl-friend were legally married and now have octuplets. Jen has been completely cleared of any medical conditions. April is six years sober and is the best-selling author of *Is Your Unorganized Utensil Drawer A Scream For Help?*"

Most people don't have a clean, clear happy ending to the traumatic events in their lives. I've had to learn to live within the trauma. Live a life while the events are happening. Get up in the morning instead of climbing in a hole and waiting for the storm to pass. Because the storm isn't going to pass while you're in the hole. I have to admit, some days, the hole is screaming, "Hey Dina! Come back!" But climbing out of it is more difficult than not going in there in the first place.

Some days I cry. Sometimes in public. But at least I am dressed, sort of, and in public. Life happens even when we're not in the mood for it. Fake a smile. Fake a courteous mood. Make some hot chocolate. Wrap yourself in a blanket and sit on the couch and watch a Will Ferrell or Chris Farley movie. If one of those two don't make you laugh, check yourself into the hospital, immediately.

When the day is really bad and I think about things in my life that have happened to me or the girls, I pray that God help me see the good. When you're in a tunnel of anger or sadness, it's hard to see good and light. I try to look for it.

The truth is that I can't sustain this kind of thing every day. But it's my goal. My heart is heavy, but movement seems to help. Laughter fights the fear.

Addicts and alcoholics are sometimes unlovable. I know this because I'm one of them. They do things and say things that make you feel sad or angry or both.

There is a saying, "Love them until they can love themselves." That's easier said than done and some days it takes all my strength. There are moments I want to say to them, "You are a fucking nut job." But I try to make a point of saying, "I love you." Even when the kids aren't acting lovable and sweet. Even if I'm not feeling the words right then, I say them.

I think, One day they will begin to love themselves, and I hope they will know the importance of saying those simple words. I'm sure there have been occasions when people told me they loved me when they wanted to tell me I was an unstable crazy mess.

Every day I make sure to tell Mom I love her. I say, "I love you, Mom." She says, "What do you mean where am I? I'm right here!"

I mean let's face it. I'm not Mother Teresa. Most days I scream the "fuck" word until sundown. But at the end of it, if nothing else, I can at least spit out an "I love you." And some days, that's as good as it gets.

There are moments when you realize what makes the world go around. Those are the moments that change your heart and you become someone else. You pray that God allows you to hold onto those moments and the people involved, and if he does, whatever else comes up, who cares? Financial problems? It's frustrating, it's stressful, but it isn't something you'll remember the day you leave the earth. It isn't so traumatic that it changes your heart. Macaroni and cheese isn't that bad. The wave will come back in.

I have a picture in my head of when we all went to Venice Beach. John and I got bikes. John's bike had a baby carriage attached to the back, and Moses sat back there like a king. The three girls got Rollerblades. I looked at them and they all grabbed each other's hands and skated off down the boardwalk. They were adults, not children. But they're sisters and they hold hands when they Rollerblade, screaming and laughing and trying not to break their necks.

I can picture Thanksgiving and taking pictures of the girls and Michael, and feeling like my heart would explode with happiness. The girls, so beautiful, and Michael, so handsome.

It's very rare, but every now and then, the girls and I manage to have lunch together.

We sit in a Mexican restaurant, and we are in a rush because Jen has a doctor's appointment for a mysterious lump on the top of her foot, which she also has on the other foot. It's called a bone, Jen.

April moves the things around on the table. "This looks bet-

ter like this, right?"

Carly says, "Do they have pasta here? I'm hungry. I'm full. I want to be a lawyer. Can I take a nap in here?"

I tell the girls, "It's okay to fight with me, but try not to fight with your sisters. One day, when you get older and your kids are driving you crazy and your husband is an asshole, you won't call me, you'll call each other. So love each other and keep each other close."

We carry on. I drink my French vanilla creamer, walk around the bookstore, kiss Moses. John plays cards. The girls do what they do to get through the day, and we keep rolling down the street.

There's another saying, "Bloom where you're planted." I'm actually a huge fan of repotting. We have choices. We don't have to follow in the path of those who came before us. Maybe the saying should be, "Bloom where you're planted, unless you've been planted on a shit farm. Then you should repot and bloom in a better area."

Carly came home after six months in rehab, and she has been clean ever since. In fact, she and Andy both have one year clean now. I pray they will be okay. Turns out, that's all I can do. Carly is clean today and all I can worry about is today. Will she stay clean? I don't know. Will April stop drinking? I don't know. Will Jen ever be happy? I have no idea. Will John run off and find a family that is not crazy? No. He doesn't even know how to arrange his pill box with the eleven different pills he takes. He's screwed without me.

So at the end of each day, I give Moses his medicine, I give

John a handful of heart pills, I give Mom her pills. And then I eat a Snickers bar and swallow it with a Coke.

Thirty-one years after my ban on religion, John and I walked through the doors of a church. It was a big, flashy church. Because we're flashy people. After thirty-one years, I needed more than your every day run-of-the-mill, give-it-to-God kind of deal.

They call the choir, and they come out and they just keep coming. There must be a hundred people. They start singing and it's like the roof is coming off. Some of them are really, really young. They're dancing and singing and the electric guitars are cutting through the enormous crowd. I think to myself, Wow, church has changed. I dig it.

I look around. The people look peaceful. They're smiling. They look calm and at home here.

I'm still filled with judgment about church and church people. I know I don't believe the same things most of these people believe. I feel because of my beliefs, I'm an infiltrator in this large group of singing and smiling people. But something comes over me. I realize that these people don't care if I'm an infiltrator or not. I sense they will take me and my group any way they can get us. We can wear a dress or jeans, dress shoes or flip flops, we can walk in or do cartwheels. These people simply don't care. They are happy to see us. We walk in, brushing off the ashes from the last thirty years. We take our seats, and I feel like we've earned these seats. Like everyone in the building, we have all earned a seat in a place where once a week we come

to replenish our spirits and let someone else be strong for us...
to come and lay everything down and be still.

We've gone every Sunday since. After John's heart attack we needed something. We've always been able to pray and keep God in our lives, but now we were weary. We needed a spiritual espresso. We needed more.

I know one Sunday morning, the pastor is going to say something that I completely disagree with. He's going to talk about the gay people, and I'm going to shift in my seat. But what I feel right now is that I need to take what I need, and leave the rest. Take what fills my heart, and leave the rest. Because really, at the end of my life if what I believe in is wrong, then I will deal with God, not this church or any church. So I guess, yes, I'm an infiltrator. And so far I'm getting away with it. I am getting spiritual enlightenment, a heart full of love, and there is a Starbucks right by the front door.

A Starbucks by the entrance of the church? Man, like I said, life is trippy. Bring out the choir. Turn it up. Let the healing begin.

Epilogue

John: You are my whole heart.

Jennifer, Michael, April, and Carly: If I knew then what I know now, I would have held you in my arms forever. I would have never let you go. I would have followed my instincts and followed my heart. I would have been more like the person I am now, but I got here by walking down a long, long road and learning everything the hard way.

Life is hard. The goal in life is not to have a life without problems and stress—because much of life is problems and stress. The goal is to continue to have faith and have a laugh.

I am a better person because of the four of you. You are the loves of my life, and I am so unbelievably proud of you. I'm thankful for all the laughter we've shared, and I'm so sorry for the times I disappointed you. But I cannot turn back the clock. And so we go on. Watching reality television and planning holidays. Laughing, crying, fighting. It's life. It's our Divine Order.

The doctor rolled the stethoscope over my stomach and then stopped. He said, "See. Right there. Can you hear it?"

I listened. Then, as clear as day, I heard your heartbeat. It was confirmation that you were with me and I was with you.

As I listened, I tried to picture you and what you would be like. And now, all these years later, I am still comforted by the sound of your heart.

About the Author

Dina Kucera was born and raised in Albuquerque, New Mexico. After completing a project to collect and identify fifty insects, she graduated from the ninth grade and left school for good. It seemed like a good idea at the time. Her first job was a paper route, and she has worked as a maid, bartender, waitress, and grocery store checker. She recently left her job as a checker to become a writer. She has also been a stand-up comic for twenty years, for which she receives payment ranging from a small amount of money to a very, very small amount of money. When it comes to awards and recognition, she was once nominated for a Girl Scout sugar cookie award, but she never actually received the award because her father decided to stop at a bar instead of going to the award ceremony. Dina waited on the curb outside the bar, repeatedly saying to panhandlers, "Sorry. I don't have any money. I'm seven." Dina is married with three daughters, one stepson, and one grandson. She currently lives in Phoenix, Arizona.